International Law
and the Resources of the Sea

International Legal Research Program
Columbia University Law School
Publications

*Legal Aspects of Foreign Investment* (W. Friedmann and R. C. Pugh, eds.), Little Brown & Co., 1959.

*Joint International Business Ventures* (W. Friedmann and G. Kalmanoff, eds.), Columbia University Press, 1961.

*International Financial Aid* (W. Friedmann, G. Kalmanoff, and R. F. Meagher), Columbia University Press, 1966.

*Government Enterprise* (W. Friedmann and J. F. Garner, eds.), Stevens and Sons, Ltd., and Columbia University Press, 1970.

*Trade Agreements for Developing Countries* (G. Verbit), Columbia University Press, 1969.

*International Law and the Resources of the Sea* (J. Andrassy), Columbia University Press, 1970.

# International Law
# and the Resources of the Sea

By Juraj Andrassy

Columbia University Press
New York and London
1970

Juraj Andrassy was Professor of International Law at the University of Zagreb for nearly four decades before his retirement in 1966. He has lectured repeatedly at The Hague Academy of International Law, and is currently the President of the Institute of International Law.

Copyright © 1970 Columbia University Press
Library of Congress Catalog Card Number: 76-130960
ISBN: 0-231-03409-1
Printed in the United States of America

# Foreword

THE PRESENT STUDY, WRITTEN BY ONE OF THE FOREMOST CON-
temporary authorities on the law of the continental shelf, deals
with one of the most important international problems of our
time. The legal status of the ocean bed is a question of far more
than legal interest. It will affect the economic balance of the
world and the very structure of international relations. The
basic issue is between the preservation of at least the most important aspects of freedom of the seas—the single most important achievement of the law of nations—and the progressive
appropriation of the ocean bed by states, and its exploitation by
competing economic interests. Inevitably, such a development
will increasingly erode the freedom of navigation and fisheries,
and immensely add to the dangers of the pollution of the oceans.

The present study is based on years of research and collab-
oration with scientists, geologists, and other experts. In short
compass, Professor Andrassy's study not only gives a survey of
the relevant facts and legal problems, but also outlines construc-
tive alternatives to the present dangerous race for the nationali-
zation of the oceans.

*Wolfgang Friedmann*
Professor of International Law; Director,
International Legal Research; Columbia University Law School

# Preface

THREE YEARS AGO I PUBLISHED A SHORT PAPER [1] DRAWING ATTEN-
tion to the advances of technology which permit man to explore
and exploit the depths of the sea, its bed, and its subsoil. Such
development has engendered thought whether coastal states
could and should extend their authority over enlarged submarine
areas on the basis of a formal interpretation of the definition of
the continental shelf as set forth in the 1958 Geneva Convention
on the Continental Shelf.

The year after this first paper, the author presented to the
Institut de Droit International a memorandum [2] proposing the
establishment of a committee to study the legal problems involved. At the same time, a similar proposal was submitted to
and accepted by the International Law Association. Also, in that
year, the present study was initiated at the suggestion of Profes-

---

1 Andrassy, "Potreba Dalje Kodifikacije Medjunarodnog Prava Mora"
("The Necessity for a New Codification of the International Law of the Sea"),
*Jugoslovenska Revija za Medjunarodno Prava (Yugoslav Review for Interna-
tional Law)*, 1965, pp. 163-75.

2 Andrassy, *Les progrès techniques et l'extension du plateau continental,
Zeitschrift für Ausländisches öffentliches Recht und Völkerrecht*, vol. 26, 1966,
pp. 698-704.

sor Wolfgang Friedmann. In the meantime, other studies were undertaken. A leading role in this respect has been assumed by the United Nations which, by Resolution 2340 (XXII), initiated a thorough study of this area in conjunction with other international agencies. Although the present study, which was begun in 1965 as a "distant early warning," will, under the circumstances, be merely one of several contributions dealing with what is today a central problem, I would be happy if it contributes to an understanding of the problems at stake.

*Juraj Andrassy*

# Acknowledgments

The author wishes to acknowledge the permission to reprint copyrighted material by the following authors and publishers:

The California Law Review, Inc. and Fred B. Rothman and Company, for permission to reprint from O. Schachter, "Scientific Advances and International Law Making," *California Law Review*, Vol. 55 (1967), pp. 423–30.

The Law of the Sea Institute, University of Rhode Island, for permission to reprint from a map, "A Hypothetical Division of the Sea Floor," prepared by Robert H. Warshing, and a note by F. T. Christy and H. Herfindal, annexed to *The Law of the Sea: Proceedings of the Second Annual Conference of the Law of the Sea Institute* (L. M. Alexander, ed., 1967).

The Ohio State University Press, for permission to print from *The Law of the Sea: Offshore Boundaries and Zones* (L. M. Alexander, ed., 1967).

The Oxford University Press, for permission to reprint from H. Lauterpacht, "Sovereignty over Submarine Areas," *British Yearbook of International Law*, Vol. 27 (1950), pp. 376–433, published for the Royal Institute of International Affairs.

# Introduction

~~~~~~~~~~~~~~~~~~~~~~~~~~~~~~~~~~~~~~~~~~~~~~~~~~~~~~~~~~~~~~~~~

THE PURPOSE OF THIS STUDY IS TO EXAMINE THE LEGAL PROBLEMS
that have already arisen and will continue to arise as technological progress permits man to explore and utilize hitherto inaccessible submarine areas. Just as man is gaining ability to travel and
communicate in outer space, he is also becoming master of the
depths of the sea and the natural resources found at the bottom
and its subsoil. Man may, in the not too distant future, use the
deep sea and the seabed for transportation, communications,
food production, the exploitation of the natural resources found
there, and other purposes.

All of these technological advances may be achieved in
stages over a long period. Each new progression into what were
formerly inaccessible or unexploitable areas will give rise to different problems. One of the most important is the question of
what legal regime should govern the newly opened areas.

The deep sea areas present problems to the world of today
analogous to those presented by the continental shelf to the
world of twenty years ago. Sir Cecil Hurst described the latter
problem as follows:

Now in the face of an increasing demand for a diminishing supply I feel—and I hope that you will all agree with me—that international lawyers must approach this subject of the Continental Shelf on a realistic basis. . . . If the world must have petroleum and petroleum is present in available quantities in the Continental Shelf, and the engineering experts say that from such sources it is a feasible proposition to obtain it, the necessary operations to obtain it will be undertaken. That is the situation which international lawyers must face.[1]

No one can say that the problems now in the limelight of the world's attention were overlooked in the past. At the time the continental shelf problem was at the fore some writers also envisaged the possibility of exploitation in submarine areas at ever greater depths and raised the question whether such areas should be governed by an international regime. This problem, however, aroused little interest in scholarly or governmental circles until the last few years. Since then a number of papers have appeared, and several discussions have been arranged by universities, other scientific institutions, and by semiofficial and official bodies including such international agencies as the Intergovernmental Oceanographic Commission. In addition, the United Nations initiated a broad study program which could, in a later stage, lead to important developments.

The Geneva Convention on the Continental Shelf consecrated the concept of the continental shelf as a principle of international law. It permitted states possessing a maritime littoral to extend their authority beyond the outer limit of their territorial sea, the hitherto traditional boundary of their sovereignty. Thus, coastal states now have exclusive rights to the seabed and subsoil of that part of the adjacent high sea where the depth is less than 200 meters, or where the depth of the superjacent waters admits of the exploitation of the natural resources of the said areas.

This extension of state authority reflects new developments

---

[1] Hurst, "Problems of Peace and War," *Transactions of the Grotius Society,* *1948,* vol. 34, pp. 158f.

caused by technological advancement. As the exploitation of sea bottom and subsoil natural resources became feasible and rewarding, various offshore activities, especially oil drilling, were taken at points beyond the limits of the sovereignty of the nearest coastal states. When these activities became more frequent and more extended, the need was felt to regulate them. Moreover, coastal states were eager to protect their own interests as well as the interests of their nationals against foreign competition and interference by other states. To justify inroads into hitherto free spaces, the first unilateral proclamations and acts claiming exclusive jurisdiction and control or, sometimes, sovereignty over areas beyond the limits of the territorial sea were based on the well-known geological and geographical concept of the "continental shelf." Claiming states contended that they derived their title from the fact that the continental shelf is a continuation of the land mass and thus of the claiming state's territory. Within a few years the concept of the continental shelf became familiar to politicians and scholars, and the matter was considered ripe for codification. Thus, within a short space of time, an entirely new concept received legal sanction.[2]

The Convention on the Continental Shelf came into force on June 10, 1964. Yet, by that time technology had already opened new areas of the oceans depths and had thereby exposed new problems which had not been explicitly considered. It will be the purpose of the present study to explore the most important of these problems, and in particular the interrelation between technological developments and the growing erosion of the freedom of the seas by expanding national claims to its resources. Thus, this study will be devoted to the various interpretations and claims derived from the Convention on the Continen-

---

[2] The Convention on the Continental Shelf, *United Nations Treaty Series*, vol. 499; p. 311, was adopted at the Geneva Conference by fifty-seven votes to three, with eight abstentions. *United Nations Conference on the Law of the Sea, Official Records*, vol. II (A/Conf. 13/38), p. 57.

tal Shelf, and to possible economic and military uses of the seabed outside and independent of the continental shelf.

This study will be divided into three parts. The first will consider the natural and technological factors which caused the current problems. The second will deal principally with the evolution of the continental shelf as a legal concept. The third will discuss various legal solutions of these problems. Part I is divided into two chapters. Chapter I will deal with marine geography and geology, especially the continental shelf. Chapter II will discuss the nature and extent of the natural resources which may be the object of exploitation, and will summarize recent technological progress.

Part II is divided into four chapters. Chapter III will consider the general trend of coastal states enlarging their jurisdiction over parts of the marine area adjacent to their coast. This trend, which began in 1945, has caused a severe change in customary international law. Chapter IV will provide a brief review of the development of the legal concept of the continental shelf and examine whether the provisions of the convention are merely a restatement of existing customary international law or whether, after their entry into force, they have become part of customary international law. Chapter V is an examination of whether the Geneva Convention on the Continental Shelf is applicable to submarine areas of the deep seas. Chapter VI deals with the problem of how boundaries between submarine areas allotted to neighboring states should be determined. Examination of pertinent provisions of the Convention on the Continental Shelf leads to the conclusion that several provisions are subject to more than one interpretation and that certain of these interpretations are not only undesirable but even improper. Thus, we must consider how to exclude or avoid an improper interpretation.

One conclusion of Part II is that the exclusive jurisdiction of individual coastal states should not extend beyond an agreed reasonable limit. Therefore, in Part III, thought must be given to a redefinition of the continental shelf (Chap. VII). Finally, Chapter VIII deals with the question of what regime should control those submarine areas not allotted to national jurisdiction. As yet, no specific rules would control the consequences of further technological advances. The lack of an adequate legal order could engender serious problems. As the Austrian delegate to the First Committee of the General Assembly, Kurt Waldheim, noted, "the existing absence of an adequate legal framework will lead inevitably, in the long run, to a race between nations seeking to establish jurisdiction over the ocean floor." [3]

A speedy solution to the problems which we have considered is essential. The general trend of states trying to extend their authority over ever increasing areas of the ocean, and individual activities trying to exploit these areas, may create situations which could grow out of hand.

---

[3] Meeting of November 14, 1967, A/C.1/PV 1527.

# Contents

Foreword                                                    v
Preface                                                     vii
Introduction                                                xi

## Part I
### *Physical and Technological Aspects of the Ocean Floor*

Chapter 1 The Physical Characteristics of the Ocean Floor   3
Chapter 2 The Resources of the Sea and Recent
        Technological Progress                                  15

## Part II
### *The Expanding Concept of the Continental Shelf*

Chapter 3 Extension of Claims to National Control Over
        Portions of the Sea                                    35
Chapter 4 The Development of the Legal Concept of
        the Continental Shelf                                  49

# Contents

Chapter 5  A Critical Examination of the Concept and
Criteria of the Continental Shelf                    70
Chapter 6  The Delimitation of the Continental Shelf in
Special Circumstances                                91


Part III
*Proposals for Revision of the Present Law*

Chapter 7  Proposals for a Redefinition of the Continental
Shelf                                               111
Chapter 8  Proposals for the Control of the Deep Ocean
Space: The Case for International Control            129


Conclusions                167
Postscript                 169
Selected Bibliography      175
Index of Cases             185
Index                      187

# Physical and Technological Aspects
## of the Ocean Floor

PART I

# 1

## The Physical Characteristics
## of the Ocean Floor

~~~~~~~~~~~~~~~~~~~~~~~~~~~~~~~~~~~~~~~~~~~~~~~~~~~~~~~~~~~~~~~~~~~~

OUR STUDY DEALS WITH SUBMARINE AREAS AND NOT WITH THE sea itself. The sea, notwithstanding the legal status of its various parts, is a physical unit which covers the greatest part (70.8 percent) of the earth's solid crust. That part of the crust which lies directly under the fluid element is known as the bottom or seabed. The soil beneath the seabed is known as the subsoil of the sea.[1] Especially for exploitation and mining purposes the seabed may be a more or less thick layer of various materials.

### Definitions of the Continental Shelf

As used scientifically, the term continental shelf refers to that part of the sea bottom which is adjacent to and surrounds all land masses; it extends from the seashore to that depth at which the seabed markedly falls off to significantly greater

---

[1] The term "seabed" is used synonymously with the term "sea bottom." Some texts use also the term "ocean floor." For example, General Assembly Resolution 2340 (XII) mentions "the sea-bed and the ocean floor, and the subsoil thereof." General terms "submarine areas" and "ocean space" are also used. Mexico proposed the term "international submarine zone" (A/C.1/L.430).

depths.[2] That part of the sea bottom where the gradient becomes steep enough to mark the limit of the continental shelf is known as the continental slope. Thus, the continental shelf is that shallow part of the sea bottom adjacent to the land. Scientists present it as an underwater base, pedestal, or shelf upon which the land mass reposes. Looked at in another way, continents are presented as land masses whose edges lie beneath the sea,[3] and the continental shelf is thought of as the submerged edge of the continents.[4]

The steeper fall-off of the seabed towards abyssal depths, beginning from the outer edge of the continental shelf, is known as the continental slope. Continuing outward is the continental rise, whose fall-off to abyssal depths is less steep. Shelf, slope, and rise form together the continental margin, or continental terrace. Recent geophysical investigations have led to the conclusion that the continental margin should be, from this point of view, considered as a whole, and intrinsically different from the rest of the ocean floor. Other authors consider as parts of the continental margin only the continental shelf and slope.

Although the continental shelf is a geological feature common to all continents, there is no uniformity.[5] There is great va-

---

[2] See the definition given by the International Committee on the Nomenclature of Ocean Bottom Features: the continenal shelf is "[t]he zone around the continent, extending from the low-water line to the depth at which there is a marked increase of slope to greater depth." "Definition of features on the Deep-Sea Floor," *Deep Sea Research*, vol. 1, no. 1, October, 1953, pp. 11–16, quoted in UNESCO, "Scientific Considerations Relating to the Continental Shelf," U.N. Doc. A/CONF.13/2 and Add. 1, para. 6 (Sept. 20, 1957); reprinted in *U.N. Conference on the Law of the Sea, Official Records*, vol. 1 (A/CONF.13/37).

[3] Stride, "The Geology of Some Continental Shelves," *Oceanography and Marine Biology*, 1, 1963, p. 77.

[4] Gilluly, Waters and Woodford, *Principles of Geology*, 1952, p. 21.

[5] The total area of continental shelves throughout the world may be estimated in two different ways. First, all areas defined as continental shelves could be isolated and measured. However, such determination would hinge on the definition used and the information available about the shelves. Al-

riety as to the depths at which the continental slope occurs, the distance from the land at which the continental slope begins, and the steepness of the gradient of the continental slope. Such diversities have an important bearing on the legal questions involved.

Some scholars define the continental shelf in terms of the depth at which the continental slope begins. For example, Julien Thoulet defines it as the "area of the sea bottom between the coast and the isobath of 200 meters or 100 fathoms." [6] Map 1 illustrates the continental shelf as delimited by the 200-meter

---

ternatively, an average depth at which the slope begins could be estimated and all sea bottom areas that are covered by columns of water of a height less than the chosen depth could be calculated. This method, which is more appropriate for our purposes since the Convention on the Continental Shelf treats as part of the continental shelf all areas inside the 200-meter isobath, was adopted by E. Kossinna in 1921. He estimated that, assuming an average depth as the limit of the shelf, the various continents have areas covered by less than the average depth in the following dimensions, expressed in millions of square kilometers:

| | |
|---|---|
| Off Europe | 3.11 |
| Off Asia | 9.38 |
| Off Africa | 1.28 |
| Off Australia | 2.70 |
| Off North America | 6.74 |
| Off South America | 2.42 |
| Off Antarctica | 0.36 |
| Off distant islands | 1.50 |
| Total | 27.49 or 7.6% of the sea surface. |

The three great oceans are part of this area:

| | Oceans (excluding Mediterranean Seas) | Mediterranean Seas |
|---|---|---|
| Atlantic Ocean | 4.59 | 9.52 |
| Indian Ocean | 2.37 | 0.80 |
| Pacific Ocean | 2.89 | 7.32 |
| | 9.85 | 17.64 |

Grand Total     27.49

These charts are reproduced in Defant, *Physical Oceanography*, 1961, I, p. 21.

[6] Thoulet, *Guide d'océanographie pratique*, 1895, p. 23.

Map 1   Continental Shelves of the World
(limited by 200 meter isobath)

isobath. Other writers have spoken in terms of the continental slope beginning at a certain average depth, adding that ". . . for convenience the 100 fathom (600 feet/183 meters) line is most often used." [7] Professor V. Zenkovitch, of Moscow, believes that it would be better to define the outer edge of the continental shelf by means of conventional isobaths of 100 to 200 meters.[8] V. J. Novák observes that it is most probable, under hitherto known data, that the depth of the marginal belt lies mostly between 100 and 200 meters.[9]

There are many examples of the continental slope beginning at lesser depths than those mentioned above. For example, Jacques Bourcart refers to the seabed of the Red Sea, 200 kilometers south of Jidda, where the sharp drop-off starts at a depth of between 50 and 80 meters.[10] Off the western Scandinavian coast the slope starts at depths between 80 and 300 meters. The broad continental shelf off northern Siberia abruptly halts at 100 meters. The Sahul Shelf off western and northwestern Australia descends to greater depths, at 300 fathoms in certain places, whereas in other places the shelf ends in quite shallow waters. In the area between 14 degrees and 22 degrees south, the sea bottom drops continually to 1,100 meters or more,[11] and in areas off the northern shores of Scandinavia the sea bottom gently descends to 650 meters without a sharp break.[12]

Just as we have noted that not all continental shelves start

---

[7] Trumbull, Technical Study presented by the United States Delegation at the Inter-American Specialized Conference on Conservation of Natural Resources, p. 1.

[8] UNESCO, *supra* note 2, at para. 53.

[9] Novák, "On the Origin of the Continental Shelf," *Věstnik Králevské ceské společnosti nauk, třida matematicko-prirodovĕcká,* 1937, XVII, p. 1.

[10] Bourcart, "Note sur la définition des formes du terrain sous-marin," *Deep-Sea Research,* Vol. 2, January, 1955, pp. 140–44.

[11] Novák, *supra* note 9, at pp. 2–3. Bourcart, *Géographic des fonds des mers,* 1949, p. 224, considers that there is no continental shelf at all.

[12] More details on this point may be found in UNESCO, *supra* note 2, at paras. 14–28.

their slope at the same depth of water, we must also observe that not all shelves have the same profile. Some shelves drop to ocean depths in two or three steps. In other areas, such as the Pacific coast of South America, a sharp fall begins at the shoreline or within a few kilometers of it.[13] A third form, which occurs in the Barents Sea and in the Sea of Okhotsk,[14] consists of shelves which abruptly descend from the coast to depths of 150 to 250 meters—the depth at which most shelves begin to fall off—and then level off into a broad flat platform.

Important differences with regard to the physical appearance of continental shelves exist as to the width of the shelf. Sources differ as to the average width of the continental shelves.[15] Some shelves, such as the ones off the western coast of South America and off the eastern coast of the Philippine Islands, only extend a few miles from the shoreline. Others, such as those off the eastern coast of Asia, the northern coasts of the Indonesian Archipelago, Australia, the British Isles, Siberia, and the coast of the Bering Sea, extend hundreds of miles. Thus, some states have no continental shelf beyond the limits of their sovereignty, whereas others have extensive areas of shelf beyond their territorial sea. As a general rule, abruptly descending littorals have narrow continental shelves, while those having a flatter profile have broad continental shelves.

As noted in the beginning of this chapter, the continental shelf is often defined as that portion of the sea bottom which lies between the coast and the first sharp fall-off to substantially

---

[13] This phenomenon explains why certain Latin American states hold extreme views on the extent of their control of the adjacent ocean.

[14] UNESCO, *supra* note 2, A/CONF.13/2/Add.1 at p. 2, A/CONF.13/37 at para. 53.

[15] Thirty miles by Sverdrup, Johnson, and Fleming, *The Oceans*, 1957, p. 21; Gilluly, Waters, and Woodford, *Principles of Geology*, 1952, p. 22; and Franklin, *The Law of the Sea: Some Recent Developments*, 1961, (U.S. Naval College, International Law Studies, 1959–1960), p. 17; forty-four miles by Fairbridge, *The Encyclopedia of Oceanography*, 1966, p. 202.

greater depths. Many writers, emphasizing the element of "fall-off," argue that in regions in which the sea bottom descends slowly but never reaches an abrupt fall-off, e.g., the Persian Gulf, there is no continental shelf. The exclusion of such areas has presented one of the difficulties in framing the legal definition of "continental shelf." The International Law Commission sought to include such areas in its definition. Thus, the legal and scientific references to "continental shelf" are not identical. As the UNESCO Secretariat noted:

Finally the existence should be noted of shallow areas between islands and/or continents. These areas incontestably form parts of the continental shelf. In some cases the islands form the raised margin of the continental shelf (e.g. Farilhoes off Portugal, Taiwan off China, Aru Islands south of New Guinea). In other cases the area can be considered a flooded part of the continent (e.g. Gulf of Paria; Baltic; White Sea; North Sea; Persian Gulf; sea between Sunda Isles, Malacca and Gulf of Siam; Yellow Sea; Gulf of Tartary; sea between New Guinea and Australia). Those areas merge imperceptibly and without any change in character morphologically or geologically with the adjoining shelves facing the wide oceans. Hence, *no doubt can arise as to their belonging to the shelf.* [Emphasis added.] [16]

Scientists are not in agreement about the origin of the continental shelf. According to some authors, such as F. V. Richthofen, Emile Haug, and J. Y. Buchanan, the continental shelf was formed by sea abrasion. Other scientists, such as John Murray, argue that the shelf was caused by sedimentation of materials that came from the land. Alfred Wegener's theory on the formation of the continents explains the continental shelf as the edge of the continental sial mass which, under the weight of the conti-

---

[16] UNESCO, *supra* note 2, para. 12. See also United States Department of State, Office of the Geographer, *Sovereignty of the Sea*, 1965, (Geographic Bulletin Series, No. 3) p. 7: "The Persian Gulf . . . is nowhere deeper than 50 fathoms. Its seabed qualifies in its entirety as a continental shelf."

nental sima, sank under sea level. V. J. Novák and Jacques Bourcart believe that a rising sea level caused by the melting of glaciers covered a gently sloping coastal land mass that had been caused by a lengthy period of erosion and abrasion. Another theory, offered by UNESCO's expert group, is that different types of the continental shelf stem from different causes.[17]

## Oceanic Shallows and Elevations

In this context we must mention oceanic shallows and elevations. They are found in all oceans. Shallows are areas found both in the midst of the ocean and near land, but they are always separated from the continental shelf by deep waters. Seamounts are elevations rising from the ocean floor. Some shallows and mounts have been known for some time, whereas others have been discovered only recently, when more exact bathymetric measurements were taken of ocean depths. Examples of shallows include the long-discovered Saya de Malha in the western portion of the Indian Ocean; an extended shallow of about 150 kilometers located east of the islands of Revilla Gigedo, in the Pacific; extended banks near the southern tip of South America, such as the Burdwood Bank to the east, and another to the southwest of Tierra del Fuego; and the Cortes Bank, which is located 50 miles beyond San Clemente Island, or 110 west of San Diego, California. The Cortes Bank, whose minimum depth is two fathoms, is separated from San Clemente Island by waters with a maximum depth of 1,400 meters, and San Clemente is separated from California by waters with a maximum depth of 1,200 meters.[18]

---

[17] UNESCO, *supra* note 2, at para. 18. For more details they refer to Shepard, *Submarine Geology*, 1948; Kuenen, *Marine Geology*, 1950; Bourcart, *Géographie du fonds des mers*, 1949; Guilcher, *Morphologie littorale et sousmarine*, 1954.

[18] Griffin, "The Law of the Sea and the Continental Shelf." Address delivered before the International Academy of Trial Lawyers, February 17, 1967.

Newly discovered shallows include the Genista Bank, which is located 13 miles southwest of Ras Jajir on the southern coast of Arabia,[19] and Hall Bank, which was discovered in 1957, is located between Madagascar and the coast of Mozambique.[20] An example of a recently discovered seamount is Vema, which was discovered by the United States research ship of that name, 500 miles off the coast of Southwest Africa. Its summit is 30 to 40 fathoms below the ocean surface, and its small peak rises to 14 fathoms below the surface. It is not directly connected with the mainland.[21] In the North Pacific, French Frigate Shoals, which are located 400 miles from Hawaii, and a series of seamounts interspersed with shallows and tiny islands extend in the direction of Midway Island.[22]

Some shallows, such as those in the Caribbean Sea surrounding the islands of Pedro and Saranilla, are found adjacent to, and surround, tiny islands. Other shallows, such as Misteriosa, which lies between the Cayman Islands and British Honduras, and Rosalind, which lies between Jamaica and the Mosquito Coast, are separated from the nearest shoreline by fairly deep water. Still other shallows, such as Aves Bank, are adjacent to uninhabited islands at one end, but separated by deeper waters

---

19 It is a roughly eliptical bank, rising from depths of 400-500 fathoms in the north, to a depth at the summit of 103 fathoms and then falling off to a depth of 900 fathoms in the south. Hall, "Survey of a Newly Discovered Feature (*Genista Bank*) off the Arabian Coast," *Deep-Sea Research*, vol. 2, 1954, p. 80.

20 Hall, "Banc Hall—Nouveau guyot dans le Canal de Mozambique," *Revue hydrographique internationale*, 1967, pp. 31-33 (English edition entitled *The International Hydrographic Review*).

21 Mallory, "Exploration of the 'Vema' Seamount," *The International Hydrographic Review*, 1966, pp. 17-23, Hull, "The Political Ocean," *Foreign Affairs*, vol. 45 April, 1967, p. 499.

22 These seamounts, with their minimum depth indicated in parentheses, include Mellish (64 m), Kinmei (10 m), Kanmu (160 m), Kuryaku (164 m), and Milwaukee (6 m). All are located between 30 degrees and 40 degrees north latitude.

from the next land mass at the other end.[23] Among the banks in the Mediterranean Sea the largest one is Banco Medino, to the southeast of Sicily.

As there is no contiguity to any offshore part of the continental shelf, both in its natural and in its legal sense according to the definition laid down in the 1958 Geneva Convention, no state may claim jurisdiction, that is, "sovereign rights," over such shallows and seamounts. Consequently, the regime established by the Geneva Convention does not apply. Therefore, when activities with respect to natural resources of the seabed and subsoil in isolated shallow parts of the ocean (which are by now accessible for exploitation by already available means and proceedings) take place, there will be a need for specific regulations.[24] The fact that such activities are likely to commence in the very near future speaks in favor of an early solution of the problems which are dealt with in the present study.[25]

In conclusion, it might be helpful to consider the following chart which expresses the percentage of the ocean floor existing at a given depth in order to appreciate the minute amount of the sea floor that has already been explored and exploited and realize what great treasures still await us:

---

[23] Only shallows whose superjacent water is less than 200 meters have been considered. The number of such known elevations will increase with the progress in oceanographic soundings. Their number increases in greater depth. Menard, "Geology of the Pacific Floor," *Experientia*, vol. 15, pp. 205–13, produces a list of 1,400 seamounts in the Pacific Ocean alone and affirms that this is but 10 per cent of existing but not yet discovered seamounts rising above the sea floor of the Pacific.

[24] See mention of that problem in the *Ad Hoc* Committee Report to the General Assembly, A/7230, Annex I, No. 5 i/ , and Annex II, No. 16, as well as the statement made by the Yugoslav delegate at the General Assembly First Committee, October 31, 1968, A/C.1/PV 1593.

[25] The urgency of the problem was stated by Senator Pell in a speech before the United States Senate on March 5, 1968, by which he introduced his draft of the Ocean Space Treaty. In this he mentioned some examples of isolated seamounts where plans have been made to create artificial islands. *Congressional Record*, vol. 114, p. 5181.

## Physical and Technological Aspects of the Ocean Floor

| Depth of the Sea in Meters | Area in 000 Km² | Percent of the Ocean Floor | |
|---|---|---|---|
| −200 | 27,123 | 7.49 | (7.6) |
| 200–1,000 | 16,012 | 4.42 | (4.3) |
| 1,000–2,000 | 15,844 | 4.38 | (4.2) |
| 2,000–3,000 | 30,762 | 8.50 | (6.8) |
| 3,000–4,000 | 75,824 | 20.94 | (19.6) |
| 4,000–5,000 | 114,725 | 31.69 | (33.0) |
| 5,000–6,000 | 76,753 | 21.20 | (23.3) |
| 6,000–7,000 | 4,461 | 1.23 | (1.1) |
| 7,000–8,000 | 380 | 0.10 | — |
| 8,000–9,000 | 115 | 0.30 | (0.1) |
| 9,000–10,000 | 32 | 0.01 | — |
| 10,000–11,000 | 2 | 0.00 | — |

# 2

## The Resources of the Sea
## and Recent Technological Progress

~~~~~~~~~~~~~~~~~~~~~~~~~~~~~~~~~~~~~~~~~~~~~~~~~~~~~~~~

THE SEA, WHICH COVERS MOST OF THE EARTH'S SURFACE, IS A BIG
depository of natural resources and the most important medium
of communications. Since time immemorial, man has harvested
such natural riches of the sea as fish, salt, and other species of
life, such as coral and sponge. Today, however, harvesting techniques have been improved to such an extent that many other
natural resources may be recovered. Until modern times these
resources have remained virtually untapped. The purpose of this
chapter is to consider the type and extent of natural resources
available in the sea, its bed, and subsoil. Such considerations are
relevant to the central questions of our study: how far coastal
states are permitted to extend their sovereign rights according to
Article 1 of the Convention of the Continental Shelf, how
should submarine activities and exploitation be regulated, and
which regime should supervise this regulation.[1]

---

[1] When considering these problems it is helpful to make the following
distinctions:
(1) Exploitation of natural resources
    a. Living resources
    b. Non-living resources

An authoritative definition of the natural resources of seabed and sea subsoil can be found in the Convention on the Continental Shelf. Article 2, Paragraph 4, of that Convention explains that natural resources

consist of the mineral and other non-living resources of the seabed and subsoil together with living organisms belonging to sedentary species, that is to say, organisms which, at the harvestable stage, either are immobile on or under the seabed or are unable to move except in constant physical contact with the seabed or the subsoil.

While this chapter will not deal with the special problems associated with sedentary fisheries, certain comments on that practice are in order. Such kind of exploitation has been widely practiced since ancient times in almost all shallow coastal waters. In some regions the harvesting grounds were located so far from shore that they extended beyond the limits of the territorial sea of the coastal state. Thus, the running of these activities led to some of the earliest extensions of a coastal state's exclusive rights beyond the limits of its territorial sea. For example, Ceylon claimed exclusive rights beyond the limits of her territorial sea with respect to pearl oysters and chanks, and Tunis, with respect to sponges. Sedentary fisheries are also important because some natural resources harvested by means of such fisheries may someday become important products of sea farming or aquiculture.

---

    (i) Extracted from the sea (in-solution mining);
    (ii) Harvested from the bottom (on-bottom mining);
    (iii) Extracted from the subsoil (in-bottom mining).
  (2) Exploitation of natural resources developed by processing or production, e.g., fish and oyster farming.
  (3) Activities conducted in the deep sea, seabottom, and subsoil:
    a. Communications
    b. Marine environment research
    c. Security and weather forecasting services
    d. Military

## Subsoil Resources of the Sea

Many resources are today extracted from the subsoil of the sea. The best known of these are oil, natural gas, and sulfur. A significant amount of the crude oil and natural gas drilled today comes from offshore wells.[2] As mankind's needs rise, a fear that existing oil deposits will be rapidly exhausted has grown. New explorations have uncovered new deposits, thereby increasing known reserves.[3] In addition, searching for new deposits also stimulates searches for improved drilling and exploitation techniques so that in the near future it may be possible to drill in deeper water areas.[4] The problems involved in the exploration and exploitation of natural gas are similar to those involved in finding and extracting oil.

Large amounts of sulfur are recovered from subsoil off the coast of Louisiana by means of the Frasch process. This technique, which is based on the fact that sulfur becomes liquid at

---

[2] In 1958, offshore oil production represented 2.3 percent of the total oil production of the United States; in 1964 the percentage rose to 6.2. During the same period offshore gas production rose from 1.2 to 4.0 percent. *Marine Science Affairs* (First Report of the President to the Congress on Marine Resources and Engineering Development, 1967), p. 145. In 1968, offshore oil production rose to 16 percent of the total oil production. By 1980, offshore wells would supply about 30 to 35 percent of the world market for petroleum.

[3] In 1938 oil production was less than 250 million tons and proven reserves were over 4 billion tons. In 1960, production exceeded one billion tons, and proven reserves were in excess of 40 billion tons. Odell, *The Economic Geography of Oil*, 1963, pp. 4–5. In 1968 total world production of oil slightly exceeded the 2 billion ton mark. *Petroleum Press Service*, January, 1969, p. 13. Proven oil reserves at the end of 1968 were valued at more than 65 billion tons, and proven gas reserves at 1,332,720 billion cubic feet. *Oil and Gas Journal*, December 30, 1968, p. 103. In 1969 the oil production reached 2,130 million tons. *Petroleum Press Service*, January, 1970, p. 5.

[4] Theoretically, oil may be found at depths of 62,620 feet in sandstone, and 51,300 feet in limestone. Cloninger, "How Deep Oil and Gas May be Expected," *World Oil*, Vol. 130, No. 6, May, 1960, p. 60. The ship *Glomar Challenger* encountered oil and gas shows in water 11,753 feet deep in the Gulf of Mexico and has since drilled in even deeper water.

temperatures between 116 and 168 degrees centigrade, involves a three-stage process. Wells must first be drilled into the deposit. Hot salt water is then pumped down to melt the sulfur. Compressed air finally forces the liquid sulfur to the surface.[5]

## Minerals on the Surface of the Seabed

Let us now consider those minerals lying on the surface of the seabed. Most of these minerals were deposited in a sedimentation process that extended over considerable periods of time. A sedimentary layer may be hundreds of meters thick. Surface deposits have also existed in the shape of nodules and as coatings of rock. Surface deposits of various minerals may be found all over the ocean and are quite rich. For example, manganese nodules, which contain manganese, iron, cobalt, copper, nickel, and lead, are found in all oceans, and their estimated volume is substantially more than one trillion tons.[6] Large quantities which could be produced are likely to have an effect on the market prices. It has been estimated that at medium levels of output, the amount of manganese thrown on the market by a single firm would be

---

[5] This process is named after Hermann Frasch who first introduced the method in Louisiana in 1895.

[6] In his speech to the First Committee of the General Assembly, Ambassador Pardo of Malta observed that the nodules "contain 43 billion tons of aluminum equivalent to reserves for 20,000 years at the 1960 world rate of consumption as compared to known land reserves for 100 years; 358 billion tons of manganese equivalent to reserves for 400,000 years as compared to known land reserves of only 100 years; 7.9 billion tons of copper equivalent to reserves for 6,000 years as compared to only 40 years for land; nearly one billion tons of zirconium equivalent to reserves for 100,000 years as compared to 100 years on land; 14.7 billion tons of nickel equivalent to reserves for 150,000 years as compared to 100 years on land; 5.2 billion tons of cobalt equivalent to reserves for 200,000 years as compared to land reserves for 40 years only; three quarters of a billion tons of molybdenum equivalent to reserves for 30,000 years as compared to 500 years on land. In addition, the Pacific Ocean nodules contain 207 billion tons of iron, nearly 10 billion tons of titanium, 25 billion tons of magnesium, 1.3 billion tons of lead, 800 million tons of vanadium, and so on." Meeting on November 1, 1967, A/C.1/PV. 1515, p. 17.

so large that the price might drop from 90 cents per unit to 50 cents per unit; the price of cobalt might drop from $1.50 per pound to $1.00; and that of nickel from 70 cents to 65 cents.[7] Other large deposits include red clay, calcareous oozes, and phosphorite nodules. Red clay covers 40 million square miles of seabed, has a volume of at least 10 quadrillion tons, and contains at least 10 trillion tons of aluminum and 10 billion tons of copper. Almost 50 percent of the ocean floor, or some 50 million square miles, contain rich quantities of calcium, carbonate, and barium sulfate. Major deposits of phosphorite nodules have been found off the coasts of Peru, Chile, Mexico, Argentina, Spain, South Africa, Japan, and both the Atlantic and Pacific coasts of the United States. Deposits discovered off the coast of California are expected to yield as much as 100 million tons of phosphorite.[8]

Although the above mentioned resources are the object of possible future exploitations, some deposits are actually mined. For example, iron ore has been mined off the coast of Japan; tin off the coast of Malaysia; diamonds off the coast of South Africa; thorium sands off the coast of south India; and sand and gravel off the coasts of several countries. Platinum dredging off the coast of the United States produces an annual income of a million dollars;[9] beach mining in Australia produces 95 percent

---

[7] Brooks, *Low-Grade and Nonconventional Sources of Manganese,* 1966, p. 105.

[8] For more details see Mero, "The Sea as a Source of Insoluble Chemicals and Minerals," Symposium of the American Chemical Society, April 2–3, 1963; Mero, *The Mineral Resources of the Sea,* 1965; Cruickshank, "The Compilation of Data on Marine Mineral Resources from Sea Floor Photographs and Bottom Samples," *Ocean Science and Ocean Engineering,* 1965, pp. 24–44; and the fascinating review given by Ambassador Pardo (Representative of Malta) to the First Committee of the General Assembly on November 1, 1967. A/C.1/PV. 1515 and 1516. Many details are given in the reports prepared by the Secretary-General. See U.N. Docs. E/4449, with Add. 1 and 2; E/4487.

[9] Science Advisory Committee to the President, *Effective Use of the Sea: Report of the Panel on Oceanography,* 1966, at p. 125. [Hereinafter cited as *Effective Use of the Sea.*]

of the rutile found in the Western world, and 80 percent of the zircon.[10]

## Minerals Suspended in the Sea

A further great source of natural resources is the sea, which holds many dissolved minerals. Although the concentration of these minerals per unit of water is small, the total quantity that is contained in sea water would reach quite large proportions.[11] Sea water, too, may become an important source for mankind's increasing need for fresh water.

## Sea Farming

Another important source of natural resources, not considered in the Geneva Convention, is sea farming. This activity can be carried on both in the sea itself and on the seabed. Kelp production off the California coast has been developed to the point where 160,000 tons are annually harvested. Thus, protein food may be produced from algae in sufficient quantity to meet inexpensively the protein demands of an ever more populated world. Another example, of a different order, is Japanese pearl production and oyster farming. Improved techniques now permit farmers to harvest 32,000 pounds of oysters per acre, as opposed to the 600 pounds per acre yielded under former methods. The opportunities that aquiculture presents are only now being understood. For example, the United States Public Health Service has identified 10 million acres of sea as suitable for shell fish farming. Assuming production to be at the conservative rate of 600

---

[10] Forest Shumway, President, Signal Oil and Gas Company, in *Undersea Technology*, April, 1967, p. 30.

[11] "Lesser amounts of sodium, calcium, and potassium compounds being recovered as by-products of extraction processes. With the development of improved desalting techniques, the chemical industry is looking to sea brine for possible new commercial opportunities." *Marine Science Affairs, supra* note 2, at p. 78.

pounds per acre, 6 billion pounds of fish would be annually produced, or a figure equal to the entire present fish catch in the United States.[12] Thus, here too is an activity that needs regulation.

## Military Uses of the Seabed

Finally, we must consider the military uses of the sea. For thousands of years, the surface of the sea has been used as a battleground for naval warfare. After the invention of the submarine the underwater area also became involved in warfare. Today, new devices are being developed to take the fighting arena down to the seabed. We hear of mine defense, torpedo defense, and defensive acoustic warfare.[13] An underwater acoustic lens system has been designed to operate at a depth of 12,000 feet, and prototypes are already being tested.[14] Antisubmarine sensors designed to detect, classify, locate, and track submarines have been developed. These sensors include active and passive sonar, magnetic anomaly detection, and radar that can work in a complex ocean environment. Nuclear submarines and submarine-based missile forces exist too. A deep submergence system project has been designed by the United States Navy which will make possible the deep-diving search and recovery of vehicles.[15] Communication and storage facilities and bases may be located on the seabed or in the subsoil (Rocksite project). These new military devices and techniques have stimulated many technological advances, especially in the area of improved diving techniques and more versatile and efficient submersibles. They also

---

[12] Galton, "Aquiculture is More Than a Dream," *The New York Times Magazine*, June 10, 1967, p. 13.

[13] "Gulf Coast Diver's Haven," *Undersea Technology*, July, 1967, pp. 29–32.

[14] "Soundings" *ibid.*, March, 1966, p. 11.

[15] By 1975 experts foresee the possibility of conducting complex, highly technical operations on the ocean bottom which are well beyond the limits of present technology. *Effective Use of the Sea, supra* note 9, at pp. 31–39.

have been defended as being of a defensive nature. However, when defense is needed, offensive weapons must already exist or at least be projected. Moreover, most defensive weapons can be used offensively. Thus, here too is an activity that needs early regulation.[16]

## Recent Technological Developments

In 1958 when the Geneva Conventions on the Law of the Sea were drafted, it was assumed that further technological developments would be relatively slow. In fact, advances have since been made at a far quicker pace than could be foreseen on the basis of then existing technology. Today one can safely prophesy that within twenty years man should be fully able to use the sea, seabed, and subsoil for many purposes. Of course, to do this he will have to develop various tools, machines, and installations. We shall now briefly review recent technological achievements and some of the advances expected in the near future. We do not purport to summarize all developments, as unforeseen techniques and devices are constantly being perfected.

*Surface Offshore Drilling.* At the present time, public interest in exploitation technology is primarily focused on the installations and devices developed for offshore drilling of oil and natural gas.[17] Originally, drilling was undertaken in modest depths

---

[16] The debates of the First Committee of the United Nations General Assembly reveal that between 1971 and 1972 thirty-one submarines capable of carrying Poseidon missiles with 10 nuclear warheads apiece could be in operation, and there is a possibility that by that date remote control nuclear weapons could be installed on the ocean floor. Meeting on November 14, 1967, A/C.1/PV. 1528, pp. 29–30, 39.

[17] Bilderbeek, "Offshore Exploration, Drilling and Development," Paper No. 13, by the Netherlands delegation, in *Proceedings of the Third Symposium on the Development of Petroleum Resources of Asia and the Far East,* Tokyo, November, 1965 E.C.A.F.E., Mineral Resources Development Series No. 26, E/CN.11/750.; Coene, "Profile of Marine Resources," paper prepared

near the shore. Thus, the techniques used on land could be applied. As the offshore drillings progressed to greater depths, the basic onshore methods were substantially refined, but never fundamentally changed. Offshore drillings were carried out from platforms which either floated on the sea's surface [18] or were sufficiently elevated over the surface so as not to be exposed to currents and waves. Today drillings are carried out from different forms of platforms: submersibles or "sit-on-bottoms" units, self-elevating platforms, surface vessel units, catamarans, and semisubmersible platforms. Multiwell drilling platforms have even been developed so that several wells may be drilled from the same platform. The depth at which drillings actually occur or are feasible has grown from year to year.[19] However, what-

---

for the Conference on Law, Organization, and Security in the Use of the Ocean, Columbus, Ohio, March, 1967.

[18] Floating units are kept on location either by anchoring them or by dynamic positioning systems. Jean Berne, *"Ancrage Dynamique,"* Conference on Petroleum and the Sea, 1965, Paper No. 120.

[19] Under-Secretary Charles F. Luce, United States Department of the Interior, in an address at the American Bar Association National Institute on Marine Resources (June 8, 1967) stated that "[o]il is currently produced in water as deep as 285 feet, and the capability to produce at greater depths exists. A platform recently completed in the Netherlands will be able to drill to 15,000 feet while resting on bottom in 135 feet of water, or while afloat in 600 feet." House Comm. on Foreign Affairs, *Interim Report on the United Nations and the Issue of Deep Ocean Resources,* House Report No. 999, 90th Congress, First Session, 1967, p. 231. The same figure of 285 feet is given by Coene, *supra* note 17, at p. 7, but he mentions a type of semisubmersible, column-stabilized rig mooring with cable, chain, and anchors, capable of drilling "today" in water depths to 1,000 feet. The following information was given in March, 1968, by the Bureau of Mines, Washington, D.C.: "A successful oil well was completed off the coast of Louisiana in a water depth of 349 feet; in 1965 a dry hole was drilled in water depth of 632 feet in the Pacific off the coast of California; core holes of limited penetration depths were drilled, for exploratory purpose only, in water depths of 4,900 feet off the Northeast coast of the United States." The United States delegate in the Economic and Technical Sub-Committee of the United Nations Committee on the Peaceful Uses of the Sea-bed stated that exploratory well drilling in deep water was being extended, and plans were under way to carry out exploratory drilling at water depths of up to 2,000 feet. Meeting of March 12, 1969, A/AC.138/SC.2/SR.2.

ever the technological potential of the platform drilling method, it does have economic limits.[20] Surface drilling installations are expensive and are exposed to risks from natural catastrophes, collisions,[21] and defects in construction, positioning, and maintenance. Storms and rough water have resulted in approximately 25 million dollars worth of drilling rig losses and damage costs over the last ten years.[22] Dramatic examples of rig losses include the loss of drilling rig "Sea Gem" in December, 1965, and the drifting away during a heavy storm of the rig "Sea Quest" in January, 1968.[23]

*On-Bottom Mining.*     To counteract the great expense of platform drilling, which substantially increases as water depth increases, the offshore drilling industry intends to develop and use underwater oil storage tanks and a completely submersible drilling installation which will be placed on the sea bottom.[24] A design for an ocean bottom drilling rig, usable in all seasons in waters ranging from 30 to 600 feet, was mentioned at the 1965 Monte Carlo Conference on Petroleum and the Sea.[25] Such rig,

---

[20] Only the technical possibility for industrial drilling is considered here. The Mohole project has already shown that deep water drilling has almost limitless feasibility. "Technically, platforms can be built to operate at very great depths. The limits are economic. Thus it is already feasible to drill beyond the continental shelves, in waters deeper than 600 feet. But the sole objective of exploration is to discover commercial reserves and, if drilling is to be justified, the means must exist to develop such reserves and bring them to market economically." *Petroleum Press Service*, 1966, p. 58.

[21] According to Griffin ("Routes maritimes à travers les champs pétrolifères du Golfe de Mexique," *Revue hydrographique internationale*, vol. 44, 1967, p. 195) in the past few years there were forty-eight collisions between ships and oil installations.

[22] Shumway, *supra* note 10, at 30.

[23] According to the London *Times* of January 16, 1968, the "Sea Quest" was built at Belfast in accordance with an American design specifically tailored to withstand hurricane conditions like those experienced off the Mexican coast.

[24] Lacy & Estes, "How New Underwater Oil Storage Units Work" *World Oil*, March, 1960, pp. 92–96; "Under Water Storage," Conference on Petroleum and the Sea, 1965, Paper No. 123.

[25] Young, "A Conceptual Design Analysis of a Completely Submersible

though, will not become workable until several needed innovations, including the improvement of diving techniques, are perfected.[26] It is hoped that sea floor operations will substantially lower expenses.

A panel of experts has anticipated slightly different developments. They summarize their findings as follows:

The consensus of oil companies is that by 1975, if technology is available, most stationary installations will be on the bottom of the sea, not on the surface. Most drilling will probably be conducted from the surface, but oil well operations and some temporary storage facilities will be on the bottom. Presently, we do not have the technology for building installations on the ocean floor, but oil companies are determined to attain it. They have estimated that about 10 years will be required to develop the technology and operating experience. . . .

. . . Since oil and mining companies expect by 1975 that some operations will be conducted in depths beyond 1,500 feet, there will be transition from divers to unmanned vehicles or manned instrumental platforms. . . .

. . . At . . . depths [beyond 1,000 feet] the diver will be replaced with highly instrumented platforms capable of maneuvering sensing devices, communicating with the surface and performing useful work. The technology being developed for space application may contribute substantially to unmanned operations at depth. Very likely these platforms will be manned and will require containers at atmospheric pressure.[27]

The Committee on the Peaceful Uses of the Seabed reported [28] in 1969 that commercial exploratory drilling of hydrocarbons in water depths up to 300–400 meters had been achieved

---

Offshore Drilling Operation," Conference on Petroleum and the Sea, Paper No. 419.

[26] "Man-in-the-Sea" Studies. See *Effective Use of the Sea, supra* note 9, at 31–39.

[27] *Effective Use of the Sea, supra* note 9, at 24, 27, 28.

[28] *Report of the Committee on the Peaceful Uses of the Seabed and the Ocean Floor Beyond the Limits of National Jurisdiction,* U.N. Doc. A/7622 (1969), at p. 47.

in one area, and that work towards the development of a system with re-entry capability in deep water could be operational in the near future.

Dramatic advances have also taken place in the refinement of "on-bottom mining." Such mining, which is undertaken in several parts of the world, is performed by means of dredging. Bucket ladder dredging systems only operate at depths of less than 150 feet, but hydraulic dredges are operational, depending upon the type of material being dredged, to approximately 200 feet. Air-lift hydraulic dredges, which should become the main technique for deep-mining operations, can be used to 1,000 feet, and wire line dredges, also known as drag and grab bucket dredges, can be used for very deep waters with high current velocity and high wave motion.[29] Another innovation is the recent development of an underwater mining ship designed to mine manganese nodules at depths from 400 to 12,000 feet.[30]

Charles F. Luce, Under-Secretary of the Interior, indicated the new possibilities for collecting natural resources at great depths when he said:

There have been serious proposals to recover phosphorite nodules in areas 40 miles off the California coast in waters as deep as 1,500 feet, and to dredge manganese nodules from the Blake Plateau 300 miles off the United States South Atlantic coast in water as deep as 4,000 feet. The prospects of recovering manganese nodules at depths as great as 20,000 feet have received serious attention.[31]

However, while certain progress in the area of deep sea mining is predicted by all experts, their evaluation of its scope and pace

---

[29] The cost of wire line dredging increases as the depth of the operation increases. See Coene, *supra* note 17, at pp. 10–11.

[30] *New York Times*, August 5, 1967, p. 26, col. 6.

[31] Address by Under-Secretary Luce, House Comm. on Foreign Affairs, *supra* note 19, at p. 231. The future prospects and use of the various dredging techniques was discussed at the World Dredging Conference, New York, May 6–8, 1966.

varies. Some experts suggest that because of the high cost of equipment needed to operate at greater depths, deep sea mining will not become feasible until the remote future. Other experts, though, believe that

low cost vehicles capable of exploitation are technologically feasible and will be realized within the next two decades. This projection is based on three fundamental premises: one, that deep submersibles of the future will operate independently of the free surface; two, that materials for deep submergence will ultimately be less expensive than material now in use for relatively shallow submersibles; and three, that free-flooded deep-machinery will have been developed.[32]

Further, the elimination of surface support will provide the greatest reduction in cost in the system operation.[33] This latter approach seems more realistic for the reasons given as well as the fact that costs generally decrease as production becomes more developed.[34]

*Underwater Transportation.* Another area of progress is underwater transportation. Although the standard submarine, which was developed for warfare, is not suitable for the exploitation of the seabed and subsoil,[35] it may in the future be possible to make use of it for the transportation of people and goods. Such development of the use for submarines would be likely to require regulations. Further, recent experiments have been undertaken to develop different forms of submersibles which can be used in exploring and working the deep seas and the seabeds. A

---

[32] Craven, "Technology and the Law of the Sea," paper presented to the Conference on Law, Organization, and Security in the Use of the Ocean, Columbus, Ohio, March 17–18, 1967, p. 17.

[33] *Ibid.*, at p. 18.

[34] For example, the high cost of nuclear weapons production has been so reduced that today almost every developed country can afford to produce them.

[35] Use of the submarine as a form of transportation might, in the future, become quite common and therefore require regulation.

number of such submersibles have been constructed and tested. One type of craft cannot move on its own power but is lowered into the sea from a supporting vessel upon which it is dependent. Another is independent of surface vessels and has external tools which can be manipulated from the vessel's interior. However, at present its movement is slow and it cannot stay underwater for a long period. Certainly, though, future improvements will increase the vessel's action radius and versatility. A further development of submersibles is an unmanned vehicle which is governed by remote control, either from a land base or a ship. This vehicle will be of greatest value when drilling and dredging techniques can be undertaken at greater depths as it can perform various tasks underwater and on the seabed.[36]

Other remote-controlled devices which have been developed and used in outer space operations can be adopted for use in submarine activities, too. For example, remote-controlled robots [37] have been developed to work on the maintenance of underwater wellheads. It is expected that remote-control devices will eventually be used for all necessary work on the seabed.[38]

---

[36] Three submersible models, constructed for deep sea research, should be specifically mentioned. The smallest, Alvin, is manned by a pilot and an observer and can operate at depths of up to 6,000 feet. It has been used to recover bombs off Palomares, Spain. A larger model, the Aluminaut, can carry 3 or 4 scientists and can dive up to 15,000 feet. Loughman, "Aluminaut Tests and Trials," *Ocean Science and Ocean Engineering*, 1965, pp. 876–83. The largest model, Trieste II, descended to the floor of the Mariana Trench, which is 35,800 feet deep. Although presently the mobility and working capacity of submersibles are restricted, they should increase substantially when fuel cells are perfected. One of the small STAR (Submarine Test and Research) vehicles is now powered by a fuel cell. Also, to resist the high pressures of the great depths more durable and dependable materials will be used. "By 1970 high-strength titanium alloys will be commercially available, and in the 1975–1980 period high-strength glass and cast ceramics will come into general use. Rapid progress is also being made in composite and fiber-reinforced materials." *Effective Use of the Sea, supra* note 9, at p. 21.

[37] RUM (Remote Underwater Manipulator).

[38] Clark, "Remote Manipulation for Sea-Floor Operations," Conference on Petroleum and the Sea, 1965, Paper No. 712.

*Living in Deep Waters.*    Spectacular progress has also been made to overcome many of the problems inherent in man's living and working in deep waters. Such activities are essential if man is to adequately explore and exploit the ocean depths and seabed: mining, fishing, aquiculture. To this effect, man must overcome various obstacles of the sea environment, especially in deeper seas: high pressure, cold, and darkness. To this end, several experimental programs, the best known being the Sealab and Precontinent experiments, have sought to test man's abilities and technology advances. The first Sealab Experiment was undertaken in 1964. Its participants lived in a steel chamber 200 feet underwater for 11 days, only leaving the chamber to work on the seabed.[39] Another, in 1965, had teams of 10 men live in a 58-foot-long steel chamber that was placed on a 205-foot-deep ocean floor off the coast of San Diego, California, for 45 days.[40] The men left their quarters to work in the surrounding water and seabed. The experiment Sealab III, which was to place a chamber on the ocean floor at a depth of 430 feet, was postponed indefinitely after the death of an oceanaut during the initial descent of the chamber.[41]

Three Precontinent experiments have been conducted by Commandant J. Y. Cousteau.[42] The first took place in 1962 off Marseilles, and the second in 1963 in the Red Sea. In the last of these, carried out in 1965 off Cape Ferrat, France, a team of six oceanauts lived for twenty-three days in a chamber which was

---

[39] Bond, "Undersea Living: A New Capability," Conference on Petroleum and the Sea, 1965, Paper No. 417.

[40] See generally Marine Technology Society, *Man's Extension into the Sea*, Transactions of the Joint Symposium, Washington, D.C., January 11–12, 1966.

[41] Booda, "Navy Currents," *Undersea Technology*, July, 1967, p. 41; *New York Times*, February 18, 1969, p. 1, col. 1.

[42] Cousteau, "At Home at Sea," *National Geographic, April,* 1964, pp. 465–507; and the following papers from the Conference on Petroleum and the Sea, 1965: Alinat, "Les expériences Précontinent et leurs perspectives," Paper No. 415; Willm, "Les vehicules sous-marins habités et autonomes," Paper No. 420; and Cousteau, "Les sous-marins d'exploration," Paper No. 421.

under a pressure of eleven atmospheres, and dove to 100- to 120-meter depths while performing various tasks. They had no support from a surface vessel. Similar experiments were organized in the Soviet Union as well. Soviet scientists spent ten days 57 feet below the surface of the Black Sea in a newly designed submarine laboratory consisting of two coupled spheres.[43]

These experiments, and others already undertaken; [44] prove that a team of men can live in an underwater chamber, which they leave only to work in the deep waters, for a period of weeks. Future experiments will be aimed at proving that man is capable of working at depths as great as 1,000 feet.[45] The Panel on Oceanography, which was established as an organ of the United States President's Science Advisory Committee, foresees by 1975 the establishment of test range stations at depths of up to 6,000 feet, "and perhaps in the abyssal deep," as well as the possibility of conducting complex, highly technical operations on those parts of the ocean bottom presently beyond the limits of technology.[46]

The major obstacles now facing man's descent into the depths are compression, breathing, cold, and darkness. Studies are presently being undertaken to perfect a breathing gas which would permit descent to 400 meters.[47] To resolve decompression problems, special decompression chambers are being produced. One type is a submersible chamber which would be

---

[43] Press news, April 2, 1969.

[44] British Aircraft Corporation's Civil Technology Group developed a commercial habitat for utilization under water, which is able to operate in depths up to 500 feet. *Petroleum Times*, March 14, 1969, p. 382.

[45] Bond, *supra* note 37.

[46] *Effective Use of the Sea*, *supra* note 9, at pp. 37, 39. On the experiments of the United States Navy see Stenuyt, "The Man in the Sea Project," Conference on Petroleum and the Sea, Paper No. 423.

[47] *Petroleum Press Service*, 1966, p. 92. Experiments are now being conducted to test special mixtures of breathing gas which will permit longer stays at greater depths. Hannen, "Oxy/Helium Deep Diving Experiments and Trials," Conference on Petroleum and the Sea, Paper No. 410. Hannen notes that in 1956, during a world record dive of 600 feet, there was only five minutes of bottom time.

closed at depth, thus retaining its pressure, which would permit decompression out of the water. A diver using it would be hoisted into the chamber while still below the surface. Decompression procedures would then start while the chamber was being brought to the control ship. There the diver would be transferred to a larger chamber to complete the operation.[48] It would also be necessary to provide for protective clothing against the cold from which divers in deeper areas suffer. The problem is to combine a high degree of insulation with flexibility.[49]

Of course, technological advances have not been limited to aiding exploitation of resources. Work is being done to improve and expand underwater transportation, e.g., inaugurating navigation lines for commercial submersibles, developing underwater vehicles to aid fishing,[50] and making submarine space available for fish farming and other forms of aquiculture. In addition, new and refined techniques will enable greater amounts of fresh water to be produced and more power to be generated.

This advancing technology will, however, create many new legal problems. Several new activities will have to be regulated and additional areas of the seabed will now be capable of exploitation and may well be claimed as part of the continental shelf.

Before proceeding to an examination of the effects which this great and continuing advance of man's control over the ocean bed has on the expansion of the legal concept of the continental shelf, we will briefly survey the other ways by which states have, in recent years, extended claims to sovereignty and national control over the sections of the seas adjacent to their territories.

---

[48] Hannen, *ibid.*

[49] See Craven, "Working in the Sea," *Science and Technology*, April, 1967, pp. 57–61, with regard to breathing and cold problems.

[50] Since 1958, the Soviet Union has used a fishing submarine called *Severyanka*. They also use a one-man submarine, *Atlanta I*, which can operate at depths of 350 feet. "World's Only Fisheries Submarine," *Undersea Technology*, March, 1966, pp. 28–29.

# The Expanding Concept of the Continental Shelf

## PART II

# 3

## Extension of Claims to National Control
## Over Portions of the Sea

FOR THE PAST SEVERAL CENTURIES VARIOUS COASTAL STATES HAVE attempted to claim diverse portions of the surface of the sea. For example, Venice at one time claimed sovereignty over the Adriatic Sea; Genoa claimed the Ligurian Sea; Spain and Portugal had differences concerning the Atlantic and Indian oceans; while England, Sweden, and Denmark claimed domination over the seas around them. However, over the past two or three centuries, the Grotian ideal of freedom of the high seas has come to be universally recognized. Today, coastal states exert exclusive authority over only small belts of the sea that surround their coast. As a result of that development, it seemed that the question of delimiting the authority of coastal states over adjacent seas was definitely settled by allotting to them a relatively small portion along the coast or along the outer line limiting the internal waters, which were modest in extent. With respect to the breadth of the territorial sea, the leading maritime nations considered as accepted that it be not wider than three miles. However, this assumption was not shared by all maritime nations, as it became obvious at the Codification Conference in 1930.

These views were, however, only the reflex of the then prevailing factors and corresponded to the technological and economic factors of that period. More recently new factors have come into being due to technological and economic progress giving new impulse to a trend towards the enlargement of the sea area over which coastal states could claim sovereignty or at least a certain degree of exclusive control and jurisdiction. As a consequence of that trend, much larger portions of the sea area have in recent times, in different degrees, been subjected to the authority of coastal states.

We shall now discuss how these claims were asserted:

(1) Base Line. A first step, generally recognized, and now approved in Article 3 of the Geneva Convention on the Territorial Sea, is the use of the low water mark to demarcate the outer limit of the land mass and to serve as the base line when measuring the breadth of the territorial sea.[1] Such use of the low water mark instead of the high water mark can considerably extend the outer limits of the territorial sea.[2] Today, only Ethiopia is on record as using the high water mark as a measuring point.[3]

---

[1] Hong Kong, Japan, and Florida, for example, have extended their coastal baselines by artificially creating additional areas by means of land fills adjacent to the shore. See Reiff, in Alexander, *The Law of the Sea*, 1967, p. 268. For the most part, if such fills affect the interests of another state, the states concerned will negotiate the problem. For instance, the land fills enlarging the territory of Monaco were the subject of negotiations between France and Monaco, which resulted in an understanding between them.

[2] For example, in the Yangtze area of the China coast, high tide extends up to five miles inland. Boggs, "Delimitation of Seaward Areas Under National Jurisdiction," *Am. J. Intl. L.*, 1951, pp. 240–66, at 252.

[3] See Ethiopian Maritime Proclamation No. 1953, Article 6: "/f/ The territorial waters of Our Empire are defined as extending from the extremity of seaboard at maximum annual high tide of the Ethiopian continental coast and of the coasts of Ethiopian islands, in parallel line on the entire seaboard and to an outward distance of twelve nautical miles, except that in the case of the Dahlac archipelago the seaward limit of the territorial waters shall be that defined in Our Federal Revenue Proclamation No. 126 of 1952, and that in the case of pearl and other sedentary fisheries the seaward limit of the territorial waters shall extend to the limits of the said fisheries." *Laws and Regulations on the Regime of the Territorial Sea*, United Nations Legislative Series, ST/LEG/SER.B/6, 1957, p. 129. Cf. the reservation of the Iranian Govern-

(2) Internal Waters. Another area of expansion concerns the definition of "internal waters." This concept refers to those parts of the sea that are so closely linked with the land as to be considered integral and inseparable parts thereof,[4] and thus subject to the sovereignty of the particular coastal state that controls such land. The Grotian definition of internal waters as being *inter fauces terrae,* has been given an ever increasingly generous interpretation. The conflict between the traditional conservative approach and a more liberal one was dramatically presented in the *Anglo-Norwegian Fisheries Case,* which was argued before the International Court of Justice. Norway, which championed the expansive view, claimed the right to define her internal waters by means of straight lines drawn between distant points situated either on the mainland, or on islands along the coast, or on rocks, some of which were not above water level during high tide. The Court held [5] that Norway's claim was not contrary to international law.

This view has since been adopted, almost *in toto,* in the Geneva Convention on the Territorial Sea and the Contiguous Zone. Article 4 states that:

1. In localities where the coast line is deeply indented and cut into, or if there is a fringe of islands along the coast in its immediate vicinity, the method of straight baselines joining appropriate points may be employed in drawing the baseline on which the breadth of the territorial sea is measured.

---

ment to the phrase "and unless another boundary line is justified by special circumstances" (Article 6, Paras. 1 and 2 of the Convention on the Continental Shelf): the Iranian Government "accepts this phrase on an understanding that one method of determining the boundary line in special circumstances would be that of measurement from the high water mark." *United Nations Treaty Series,* Vol. 499, p. 343. This point was also raised by the Iranian delegation to the 1958 Geneva Conference, *U.N. Conference on the Law of the Sea, Official Records,* 1958, vol. 6 (A/CONF.13/42), at p. 142. [Hereinafter cited as *1958 Conference on the Sea.*]

4 Grotius defined them as areas *"inter fauces terrae."*

5 *Fisheries Case, Judgment of December 18, 1951, I.C.J. Reports, 1951,* p. 116.

2. The drawing of such baselines must not depart from the general direction of the coast, and the sea areas lying within the lines must be sufficiently closely linked to the land domain to be subject to the régime of internal waters.

It may be noted that the Geneva Convention did not adopt that part of the decision of the International Court of Justice allowing the straight lines to be drawn even from or to elevations which appear above the sea level only during the low tide:

Baselines shall not be drawn to and from low-tide elevations, unless lighthouses or similar installations which are permanently above sea level have been built on them.

One consequence of the approach of the *Anglo-Norwegian Fisheries Case* and the Geneva Convention is the extension of the outer limit of the territorial sea. This extension results from the fact that the baseline marking the coastal or interior limits of the territorial sea is drawn along the outer limits of the internal waters.

This concept of "internal waters" has been further liberalized by the growth of the customary international law rule that bays whose entrance from the sea do not exceed a predetermined width and whose circumference is fully encircled by one coastal state are part of that state's territory. General agreement as to the maximum width of the entrance never existed before 1958. The conservative view was that the width of the entrance should not exceed six miles, i.e., double the conservative measure of the breadth of the territorial sea. There were opinions expressed, however, in favor of permitting wider entrance and claims over even larger bays. The latter were considered to be exceptions to the general rule, under the term "historic bays." [6] Subsequently, more liberal views were expressed. The Convention for the Reg-

---

[6] Bouchez, *The Regime of Bays in International Law*, 1964, especially pp. 199–230.

ulation of the Police of the Fisheries in the North Sea (1882) recognized those bays with an entrance of ten miles or less as internal waters. In 1894 the Institut de Droit International had adopted the rule that all bays which either had an entrance of twelve miles or less, or which had been subject to continuous and centennial sovereignty, should be considered internal waters. But in 1928, a ten-mile width was adopted by the Institut and in 1929 by the Harvard Research in International Law.[7] In the 1930 Codification Conference, the participating states claimed a maximum width between six and twenty miles. The 1958 Geneva Convention on the Territorial Sea set a maximum width of twenty-four miles [8] and reserved the question of historic bays for further study.

In this context the views of some insular states, especially of Indonesia and the Philippines, should be mentioned. Both states consider the sea between their islands to be internal waters and draw straight lines between the outermost points of their insular territory as baseline from which their territorial sea is measured.[9] On December 12, 1955, the Government of the Philippines addressed notes to various countries and to the United Nations Secretariat in which it declared:

All waters around, between and connecting different islands belonging to the Philippines Archipelago, irrespective of their width and dimension, are necessary appurtenances of its island territory, form an integral part of the national or *inland* [underscoring added] waters, subject to the exclusive sovereignty of the Philippines.[10]

---

[7] Article 5 of the Draft Convention on the Law of Territorial Waters. See the *Am. J. Intl. L.*, Special Supplement, 1929, at p. 265.

[8] In their first draft, the International Law Commission proposed fifteen miles. *1958 Conference on the Sea*, vol. 2 (A/CONF.13/38), at 62, vol. 3 (A/CONF.13/39), at 160.

[9] See *1958 Conference on the Sea*, vol. 1 (A/CONF. 13/37), at pp. 298–99; and see map in *Supplement to Laws and Regulations on the Regime of the Territorial Sea*, (A/CONF. 19/5/Add. 1).

[10] *1958 Conference on the Sea*, vol. 1 (A/CONF. 13/37), at 299, *Ybk. Int'l L. Comm'n, 1956*, II, p. 70. The Philippines also claim as part of their territorial

Such measurement of the outer limits of the interior waters, i.e., the drawing of a baseline between the outermost points of the outermost islands, was defended by the Indonesian delegate to the 1958 Geneva Conference on the Law of the Sea, in the following manner:

If each of Indonesia's component islands were to have its own territorial sea, the exercise of effective control would be made extremely difficult. Furthermore, in the event of an outbreak of hostilities, the use of modern means of destruction in the interjacent waters would have a disastrous effect on the population of the islands and on the living resources of the maritime areas concerned. That was why the Indonesian Government believed that the seas between and around the islands should be considered as forming a whole with the land territory, and that the country's territorial sea should be measured from baselines drawn between the outermost points of the outermost islands.[11]

(3) Territorial Sea. The desire of coastal states to further extend their exclusive authority into the sea is also reflected in

---

waters "[a]ll other water areas embraced within the lines described in the Treaty of Paris of 10 December 1898, the Treaty concluded at Washington, D.C. between the United States and Spain on 7 November 1900, the Agreement between the United States and the United Kingdom of 2 January 1930, and the Convention of 6 July 1932 between the United States and Great Britain, as reproduced in section 6 of Commonwealth Act No. 4003 and article 1 . . . of the Philippine Constitution, are considered as maritime territorial waters of the Philippines for purposes of protection of its fishing rights, . . . without prejudice to the exercise by friendly foreign vessels of the right of innocent passage over those waters." *Ibid*. It may be observed that, as the Treaty of November 7, 1900 (Martens, *Nouveau Recueil Général de Traités* 2nd series, vol. 32, p. 82) makes clear, the international agreements referred to (see Martens, *op. cit.*, 2nd series, vol. 32, p. 74, and 3rd series, vol. 27, pp. 58 and 66) only deal with the cession of territory. The indicated geographic coordinates are only relevant in determining which islands were ceded. Neither bear upon whether the water areas so described are "maritime territorial waters of the Philippines."

11 *1958 Conference on the Sea*, vol. 3 (A/CONF. 13/39), p. 44. According to the 1951 Ecuadorean Decree on Territorial Waters, the Galapagos Islands are also considered as a closed unit. *Laws and Regulations on the Regime of the Territorial Sea*, United Nations Legislative Series, ST/LEG/SER.B/6, 1957, p. 13.

the extension of the territorial sea. Before 1930 all major maritime powers restricted their territorial sea claims to a breadth of three miles, and most writers considered the three-mile territorial sea a rule of customary international law. However, at the 1930 Hague Conference for the Codification of International Law, it became apparent that many states favored a larger territorial sea. Members of the Second Committee of the Conference informally tried to ascertain the views of the states represented. Substantial diversity of opinion existed. Eighteen states, including all the major maritime countries,[12] preferred the three-mile limit. However, eight of these eighteen states wished to add a contiguous zone so as to extend their control for certain purposes beyond the territorial sea. On the other hand, seventeen states claimed more than three miles, namely four or six.[13] The Soviet Union was only represented by an observer who expressed the view that states are free to establish the limit of their territorial sea at three, four, six, or twelve miles. Thus, by 1930, it was clear that although the major maritime powers still advocated the three-mile rule, it would never be generally accepted.[14] In this connection a writer at the time summarized the three-mile limit as "a catchword without justification . . . when used in the sense of a universally adopted territorial limit." [15]

By 1958 adherents to the three-mile limit were in a minority and the real struggle was over the advisability of a six- or twelve-mile limit. Unfortunately, no compromise was effected at the 1958 Geneva Conference, and the Convention on the Territorial Sea, as adopted, did not fix the outer boundaries of the territorial sea. While inability to settle this problem was one of the

---

[12] These countries controlled 80 per cent of the world's shipping by tonnage. Oda, *International Control of Sea Resources*, 1963, p. 14. See the list of votes in Hackworth, *Digest of International Law*, 1940, I, p. 628.

[13] *Acts of the Conference for the Codification of International Law*, 1930, vol. 3, pp. 123–25.

[14] See, on the defeat of the three-mile rule, Gidel, *Le droit international public de la mer*, 1930, III, pp. 151–52; Hudson, "The First Conference for the Codification of International Law," *Am. J. Int'l L.* 1930, p. 514.

[15] Meyer, *The Extent of Jurisdiction in Coastal Waters*, 1930, p. 514.

major failures of the conference, some limits to state control of the adjacent sea were prescribed. Article 24 of the Convention on the Territorial Sea, which permits states to proclaim a contiguous zone, prohibits this zone from extending more than twelve miles from either the low water mark on the coast line or the outward limit of the internal waters. Thus, it seems clear that the territorial sea could not be more than twelve miles wide.

A new conference was convened at Geneva in 1960 to define the limits of the territorial sea but it, too, ended without success. It seems unlikely that a consensus could be reached on any limit less than twelve miles. In 1960, fourteen states claimed a twelve-mile territorial sea; in 1967, their number increased to thirty-three. During this period the number of states claiming a three-mile limit fell from thirty to twenty-five. Also during this period, twenty-five states, including some of the staunchest advocates of the three-mile rule,[16] extended their zones of exclusive fishing rights from six to nine miles beyond the outer limits of their territorial sea, and several bilateral and multilateral agreements recognized a twelve-mile limit for exclusive fishing rights.[17]

While it would seem that the gap between various positions has been narrow, developments in Latin America dispel such illusions. In 1952, at the Santiago Conference on the Exploration and Conservation of Maritime Resources of the South Pacific, Chile, Ecuador, and Peru signed the Declaration of Santiago on the Maritime Zone, wherein they proclaimed that as a principle

---

[16] British Fishery Limits Act, 1964, 13 Eliz. II, c. 72; United States Public Law 89–658, October 14, 1966, 80 Stat. 908, 16 U.S.C.A. 1091; French Law as announced in the London *Times,* June 13, 1967.

[17] United Kingdom–Denmark, April 27, 1959; United Kingdom–Norway, November 17, 1960; United Kingdom–Iceland, March 11, 1961; United Kingdom–Poland, September 26, 1964; United Kingdom–Norway, September 28, 1964; United Kingdom–Soviet Union, September 30, 1964; European Fishery Convention, London, March 9, 1964. See *Developments in the Law of the Sea 1958–1964,* (British Institute of International and Comparative Law, International Law Series No. 3, 1965).

of their international maritime policy [18] each of them possesses sole sovereignty and jurisdiction over an area of the sea adjacent to their coast and extending to at least 200 nautical miles from said coast. A similar zone is to extend around any islands belonging to these states. A provision in the Declaration provides that the Declaration "shall not be construed as disregarding the necessary restrictions on the exercise of sovereignty and jurisdiction imposed by international law to permit the innocent and inoffensive passage of vessels of all nations through the zone." However, the three states have enforced their policy against unauthorized fishing vessels.[19]

At a conference in Lima, Peru, held in 1954, Costa Rica, El Salvador, and Honduras joined in claiming exclusive authority over 200-mile zones. At the third meeting of the Inter-American Council of Jurists, held in Mexico City in 1956, the representatives of Chile, Ecuador, and Peru attempted to justify the Santiago Declaration as a defensive measure to protect fisheries. They argued that it was not contrary to any rule of international law and did not violate the principle of freedom of the seas. A resolution was then adopted over the objections of the United States and Cuba affirming the right of coastal states to exclusive exploitation of species of fish closely related to the coast, the life of the country, or the needs of the coastal populations.[20]

Representatives of the various Latin American states, as well as a number of writers, have attempted to explain the Santiago Declaration. However, their arguments in support differ.

---

[18] This conception was first unilaterally proclaimed by Chile on June 23, 1947, and by Peru on August 1, 1947. See Whiteman, *Digest of International Law*, IV, pp. 1089–90.

[19] A well-known example is the November, 1954, seizure of ships forming part of an Onassis fishing fleet. The Commission on Marine Science, Engineering and Resources reports that in seven years fines payed by seized United States fishing vessels reached $332,702. *Our Nation at Sea*, 1969.

[20] See MacChesney, *Situations, Documents, and Commentary on Recent Developments in the International Law of the Sea*, 1957, (U.S. Naval War College, International Law Situation and Documents, 1956), pp. 247, 265–81.

The representatives of the concerned states tried to restrict the scope of the Declaration in their statement before the Sixth Committee of the General Assembly in 1956.[21] F. V. Garcia-Amador also tried to limit the coverage of the Declaration. He said that

There seems to be no ground for identifying the two hundred mile maritime zone with a territorial sea in the proper sense of the term. In the first place, this term is not used in the Declaration nor did the countries which signed it annul the legal provisions already fixing the breadth of their respective territorial seas. What is more, the purpose of the zone, as expressly stated, is to extend not the entire competence of the coastal State over the new area of the sea but merely its sovereign and exclusive competence for specific purposes up to the limits indicated . . . it [is] a *maritime zone sui generis.*[22] [Emphasis added.]

On the other hand, an expansive view of the Declaration has been advocated and used in practice. A justification for such approach has been offered by the Honduran delegate, Lopez Villamil,[23] who suggests that the concerned Latin American states have title to the seabed, subsoil, and superjacent waters extending as far as 200 miles from the coast because they have no continental shelf in the geological sense, and the natural resources in the claimed sea belt "are properly theirs *because* of geographic proximity in the nearby geobiologic region." [24] (Emphasis added.)

However, since various forms of life are related in several different ways, natural resources in any claimed area might well be geobiologically related to resources located on the adjacent

[21] Meetings on November 29, 1956, A/C.6/SR 486, p. 28; December 4, 1956, A/C.6/SR 489, p. 45; December 12, 1956, A/C.6/SR 496, p. 86; December 14, 1956, A/C.6/SR 498, p. 97.

[22] Garcia-Amador, *Exploitation and Conservation of the Resources of the Sea,* 1963, p. 77.

[23] Author of an important study on the subject, *La plataforma continental y los problemas jurídicos del mar* (1958).

[24] General Assembly, First Committee, November 14, 1967, A/C.1/PV 1527.

coastal and land mass. Thus, a coastal state's control could be extended to certain resources located even beyond the 200-mile limit.

(4) Sovereignty over the Territorial Sea. Yet another change in the concept of the territorial sea concerns the relationship of a coastal state to its territorial waters. Such writers as Albert de Lapradelle and Paul Fauchille [25] denied that the territorial sea is subject to the sovereignty of the coastal state. Lapradelle believed that the entire sea, including the so-called "territorial sea," is *res communis*, and the special rights which international law gave to coastal states were in the nature of servitudes (*faisceau de servitudes*).[26] Fauchille thought that any control exercised by a coastal state over its territorial sea derived its support from the right of conservation which in turn was based on the principle of self-preservation.[27] However, although the concept of the territorial sea as being subject to the sovereignty of the coastal state has developed to the point of general acceptance today, in 1894 the Institut de Droit International declared that a state has "some right of sovereignty" (*un droit de souveraineté*) over its territorial sea; by 1928 the Institut modified their position and adopted a resolution recognizing the full sovereignty of coastal states over their territorial sea. This change of opinion was due to the fact that several international conventions had accepted the sovereignty doctrine.[28] The recognition of the sovereignty theory in the 1930 Draft Convention on Territorial Sea was the

---

[25] For a full account see Fauchille, *Traité de droit international public,* 8th edition, 1925, vol. 1, part 2, pp. 131–72.

[26] A. de Lapradelle, "Le droit de l'état sur la mer territoriale," *Revue générale de droit international public,* 1898, vol. 5 pp. 264–84, and 309–47, especially at 309; A. de Lapradelle, *La mer,* 1934, pp. 195–212.

[27] Fauchille, *supra* note 25, p. 147.

[28] Article 1 of the Paris Convention on Aerial Navigation, 1919 (Hudson, *International Legislation,* 1931, vol. 1, pp. 359), declares the territorial sea to be a part of a state's territory. Article 1 of the Pan-American Convention on Commercial Aerial Navigation, signed at Havana on February 20, 1928, (47 Stat. 1901, T.S. 840), states that "The High Contracting Parties agree that every State has complete and exclusive sovereignty over the aerial space over its territory *and its territorial waters.*" (Emphasis added.)

demonstration of the almost general acceptance of the theory.[29] Article 1 of the Draft Convention stated that:

*The territory of a state includes* a belt of sea described in this Convention as the territorial sea. *Sovereignty* over this belt is exercised subject to the conditions prescribed by the present Convention and the other rules of international law.[30] [Emphasis added.]

However, opposing views were expressed as recently as during the drafting of the Geneva Conventions.[31]

(5) Contiguous Zone. A related concept is the notion of the "contiguous zone." This concept grew out of the belief held by many states that the relatively narrow territorial sea did not sufficiently protect all their relevant interests. Although the zone is considered part of the high seas and is subject to the principle of freedom of the seas, state controls over it are increasing. The concept is recognized both in the practice of states and in the Geneva Convention on the Territorial Sea and the Contiguous Zone. The convention indirectly attempted to limit the breadth of the zone by indicating a twelve-mile maximum width for the combined area of the territorial sea and the contiguous zone. Yet, if the tendency to increase the breadth of the territorial sea to twelve miles finds general recognition and application, it may be that claims for an additional zone will be made.

(6) Special Zones. Two recent international conventions have singled out two zones of special interest for additional protection.

---

[29] The Draft Convention was not adopted because the delegates to the drafting conference were unable to agree on the breadth of the territorial sea.

[30] *Acts of the Conference for the Codification of International Law,* 1930, vol. 1, at 126. See Hudson, "The First Conference for the Codification of International Law," *Am. J. Int'l L.* 1930, pp. 447–66, at 456.

[31] Albert and Paul de Lapradelle spoke against it at the 1950 International Law Association Conference at Copenhagen, and Georges Scelle expressed his disfavor to the International Law Commission and in a special paper, *Plateau Continental et Droit International,* 1955.

The 1954 London Convention for the Prevention of Pollution of the Sea by Oil, which was amended in 1962, provides for prohibited zones (normally 50 miles wide, but in some regions extending 100 or 150 miles from land) in which, although the coastal state has no special authority, its concern for preventing its shorelines and natural resources from being affected by oil is protected.

The Geneva Convention on Fishing and Conservation of Living Resources of the High Seas of 1958 gives the coastal state two special privileges: a right—regardless of whether its nationals fish there—to participate in any system of research and regulation aimed at conserving the living resources in the high seas adjacent to its territorial sea,[32] and a right to initiate negotiations for the purpose of preparing an agreement on the conservation of the living resources. The coastal state also has the right to initiate negotiations with a view to prescribing by agreement the measures necessary for the conservation of the living resources in the same area. If no conservation agreement is reached within six months of the start of negotiations, the coastal state may adopt unilateral measures which will be valid for other states if certain requirements indicated by the Convention are fulfilled.

Despite the development of such concepts as the "contiguous zone" and the two treaties just discussed, some states feel that their interests are still not being sufficiently protected. For example, Guinea has claimed special fishing zones extending 130 miles from its shoreline; India, Pakistan, Ceylon, and Ghana claim 100-mile-wide fishing zones; while Tunisia claims a zone of 60 miles. Many states have expressed their unwillingness to recognize these and the Latin American claims mentioned above. Thus, in January, 1967, the Soviet Union lodged a protest to Argentina stating that according to the 1958 Geneva Convention

---

[32] Other states may participate in such conservation system only if their nationals fish in the area.

the high seas are free for all nations to use and no state may claim sovereignty to any part thereof, even if such claim is limited to the control of fishing.

(7) Continental Shelf. The last and the most spectacular extension of the claim of states over areas of the open seas is the claim to exercise a kind of authority as well as exclusive rights over submarine areas, i.e., the seabed and subsoil near the claiming state's coasts, but outside the limits of the territorial sea. These areas become known by the term "continental shelf." The problems raised by these recent developments are the subject of the present study.

The conclusion which one may draw from the foregoing facts is that strong forces and tendencies are at work in extending and affirming the coastal states' authority, jurisdiction, sovereignty, and influence into the open sea as far as possible. Thus, it must also be expected that with respect to the extension or restriction of the outward limits of the continental shelf, in accordance with its definition in Article 1 of the Geneva Convention on the Continental Shelf, a strong trend in favor of an extensive interpretation will be felt.

# 4

## The Development of the Legal Concept
## of the Continental Shelf

WHILE REFERENCES TO THE CONTINENTAL SHELF COULD BE found before 1945,[1] until then it did not serve as a basis for coastal state claims over the seabed and subsoil beyond their territorial sea. Such a claim was first advanced by President Truman

---

[1] See discussion by François, *Report on the Regime of the High Seas,* A/CN.4/17, para. 22, reprinted in *Ybk. Int'l L. Comm'n, 1950*, p. 49, para. 102. In a meeting on fisheries at Madrid in 1916 Oden de Buen advocated extending coastal state jurisdiction so as to further fish conservation. Moreover, proposals to extend the territorial sea fifteen miles further into the ocean were made at various Congresses on Fisheries. See League of Nations Document C.196.M.70. 1927.V, pp. 63 and 192–93. In another context, the United Kingdom and Venezuela divided the submarine areas of the Gulf of Paria between themselves by a treaty dated February 26, 1942. The official British edition of this treaty is contained in *Treaty Series*, 1942, No. 10. François properly observed that the Proclamation of the Imperial Government, dated September 29, 1916, which extended Russian sovereignty over various islands north of Siberia because they were part of the Siberian "continental shelf" was not an application of the continental shelf concept, but was rather an application of the doctrine of contiguity. See Lakhtine, *Rights over the Arctic,* 1938, pp. 43–45, (the original Russian version is entitled *Prava na severnye polarnye prostranstva,* 1928); and an article by the same author in the *Am. J. Int'l L.,* 1930, pp. 703–17. See Franklin, *The Law of the Sea: Some Recent Developments,* 1961 (U.S. Naval War College, International Law Studies, 1959–1960), pp. 30–38.

in a proclamation issued September 28, 1945.[2] President Truman there declared that

. . . having concern for the urgency of conserving and prudently utilizing its natural resources, the government of the United States regards the natural resources of the subsoil and seabed of the continental shelf beneath the high seas but contiguous to the coasts of the United States as appertaining to the United States, subject to its jurisdiction and control. . . . The character as high seas of the waters above the continental shelf and the right to their free and unimpeded navigation are in no way thus affected.

The proclamation did not specify the outer limits of the claim. A subsequent press release, however, indicated that it was only to extend to the 100-fathom isobath.

Although it was clear that this claim constituted an inroad in an area which was deemed to be governed by the Grotian principle of the freedom of the seas, it met no open opposition. In fact, it was quickly emulated by several other states. In 1945, and in the following years, several Latin American, Near Eastern states, and others issued declarations by which they extended their authority over submarine areas outside their territorial waters. However, there was no uniformity as to the kind of authority a claiming state sought to exercise or the extent of the area it wished to control. Authority was asserted either by the Truman formula of "Jurisdiction and Control"; by claim to sovereignty; or by annexation of certain areas, and an extension of state limits. The scope of the asserted claims was generally limited to the seabed and its subsoil, and a provision was usually included which explicitly recognized the principle of freedom of the seas with regard to navigation and fishing in the superjacent waters. The few claims that attempted to include the sea itself were met with protests. The limits of the claims were expressed either

---

[2] *Dep't St. Bull.*, September 30, 1945, pp. 484–86; *Am. J. Int'l L.*, 1946, Supplement, pp. 45–47.

in terms of the depth of the overlying waters, in which case the isobath of 200 meters and 100 fathoms was generally used, or with regard to a predetermined distance from the coast, in which instance 200 miles was used.[3] All claims were based upon the argument that since the continental shelf is merely a continuation of the land mass, it is only natural that the coastal states controlling the land mass should also control its extension.[4] As we noted in the preceding chapter, these claims are another manifestation of the growing trend of coastal states to ever extend their sphere of influence into the sea.

Within a short time there was much examination of the new concept by scholars and publicists, and a substantial part of the doctrine's subsequent development is owed to the work of writers, the International Law Association,[5] and the Interna-

---

[3] See Chapter 3, *supra*, at pp. 42–44.

[4] See, for instance, Emery, "Geological Aspects of Sea-Floor Sovereignty," in Alexander, *The Law of the Sea*, 1967, pp. 139–57, at 148. This was one of the strongest arguments in support of the initial claims to jurisdiction by the coastal state over the continental shelf. Now, it may be used, and is used, in the opposite sense, i.e., against an exaggerated extension of the coastal state's rights. See *infra*, Chapter 6, pp. 96–99, a reference to the judgment in *The North Sea Continental Shelf Cases*.

[5] A major contribution to the first stage of study of the continental shelf question was made by the International Law Association. The question had been put on the agenda of the Association's conferences as early as 1948, at Brussels. After a short discussion on a paper submitted by Jonkheer Feith, the 1958 Conference decided that the study of the question on the "rights to the seabed and its subsoil" should be entrusted to a committee. *Report of the Forty-Third Conference, Brussels, 1948*, pp. x, 168–206. The Committee sent a questionnaire to national branches of the Association, and drew up, on the basis of a number of answers to the questionnaire and from statements in its own debates, a report which represented a compromise between adherents of the thesis that the continental shelf concept had already been adopted by customary international law, and the opponents of this view. *Report of the Forty-Fourth Conference, Copenhagen*, 1950, at 125–38. The Committee distinguished between rules which were deemed to be existing international law and the rules *de lege ferenda*. This report was discussed at the Copenhagen Conference of the Association (1950) where the divergence of views were clearly demonstrated. Thereupon the Committee withdrew its conclusions and the Conference referred the question back to the Committee for further study and consideration. *Ibid.*, at vi, 117. At the next conference,

tional Bar Association. Further, from 1949 to 1956 the International Law Commission, with J. P. A. François acting as special rapporteur, studied the law of the high seas. Their report and final draft articles on the continental shelf, published in 1956, served as the basis for discussion at the Geneva Conference on the International Law of the Sea of 1958. At that Conference the Convention on the Continental Shelf, which clarified the legality of claims to the continental shelf, was signed.[6]

In brief, the Convention recognizes that all coastal states have sovereign rights over the continental shelf, regardless of state proclamation or occupation, for purposes of exploring and exploiting the natural resources found thereon. It defines the continental shelf as "the seabed and subsoil of submarine areas adjacent to the coast but outside the area of the territorial sea, to a depth of two hundred meters, or beyond that limit, to where the depth of the superjacent waters admits of the exploitation of the natural resources of the said areas"; thus excluding claims to the overlying waters. Islands are also recognized as having their own continental shelf. As we can see, the legal and scientific conceptions of the continental shelf do not overlap. The legal concept, unlike the scientific one, does not begin at the shore, since the seabed and subsoil near the shoreline are subsumed under the legal concept of the territorial sea and is consequently a part of its territory.

Moreover, the continental shelf in its legal sense only ex-

---

Lucerne, a short report by François was submitted (*Report of the Forty-Fifth Conference,* 1952, pp. 164–70), but in view of various opinions expressed in the debates the whole question was referred to a new committee. A new report by Richard Young was finally adopted at the next conference, held at Edinburgh in 1954 (*Report of the Forty-Sixth Conference,* 1954, pp. 411–24).

[6] The Convention was signed April 29, 1958. It was registered with the Secretariat of the United Nations as No. 7302 and was published in vol. 499 of the *United Nations Treaty Series.* By February 6, 1970, forty-two instruments of ratification or accession were deposited. The latest was that by Canada.

tends as far as the 200-meter isobath, or to such deeper point as exploitation of natural resources is possible, whereas in its scientific sense it ends where the continental slope begins.[7] The many momentous implications of this definition and the impact of recent technological developments on the interpretation of the Convention and the freedom of the seas will be examined in later chapters. At this point it is necessary to appraise the effect of the Convention on the customary law of nations.

## *The Relationship of the Geneva Convention to Customary International Law*

The four conventions adopted at Geneva in 1958 are a remarkable work of codification of international law and constitute, after their entry into force, an important part of conventional rules governing the international law of the sea. They are binding as between the states which are parties to each of the conventions. However, as for every similar codification work, it is interesting to know how far the codified law of the sea has adopted already existing customary rules, and how far it has introduced innovations. The question how far the rules or provisions of the Convention on the Continental Shelf reproduce customary international law, or how they have become customary international law after their entry into the text of the Convention merits the reader's interest for several reasons. First, there are many states which did not adhere to the Convention, so that instead of being bound by its provisions, they are bound by customary international law. Second, a number of states have adhered to the Convention with certain reservations or expressed individual interpretations which were not accepted by other states which are parties to the Convention.

In case of differences between such states, the question might arise whether the respective provisions of the Convention

---

[7] See above, Chapter 2.

are valid between those states as part of customary international law. Finally, the question has also an important bearing upon the problems raised in the present study, namely the universal validity of the rule of Article 2 in connection with Article 1, which recognizes the right of every coastal state *ipso facto* to specific exclusive rights to areas, the exent of which might become a major cause of conflict.

The Convention on the Continental Shelf, like the other three Geneva conventions, is based upon the preparatory work of the International Law Commission. The Commission was created as an auxiliary organ of the General Assembly for performing its duties as set out in Article 13, para. 1 (a) of the Charter, concerning the progressive development and codification of international law. Article 15 of the Commission's statute uses the term "progressive development of international law" in the sense of "the preparation of draft conventions on subjects which have not yet been regulated by international law or in regard to which law has not yet been sufficiently developed in the practice of States." The term "codification of international law" is used "as meaning the more precise formulation and systematization of rules of international law in fields where there already has been extensive State practice, precedent and doctrine." Such phrasing itself indicates that there is no clear-cut limit between progressive development and codification. The practice of the International Law Commission confirms this view, which is generally recognized by the writers as well. A mere restatement of existing rules of international law occurs but rarely. The codification work achieved by the United Nations thus far combines codification of existing law and its further development.

Such a view is especially justified with regard to the 1958 Geneva Conventions. Only one of them, the Convention on the High Seas, might be said to be, at least generally speaking, a codification in the first sense. The remaining three conventions represent development and improvement of preexisting law. This can also be seen by comparing the introductory phrases of the four conventions. The Preamble to the Convention on the High Seas declares:

The States Parties to this Convention,
Desiring to codify the rules of international law relating to the high seas,
Recognizing that the United Nations Conference on the Law of the Sea, held at Geneva from 24 February to 27 April 1958, adopted the following provisions as generally declaratory of established principles of international law,
Have agreed as follows:

The three remaining conventions that were adopted and signed at Geneva, including the Convention on the Continental Shelf, do not use that formula. Instead, the Convention on the Territorial Sea and the Contiguous Zone, and the Convention on the Continental Shelf state very briefly:

The States Parties to this Convention
Have agreed as follows.

Thus, the Preamble to the Convention on the Continental Shelf, when read together with the Preamble to the Convention on the High Seas, might be considered to imply that new law was being created. The analysis which follows should demonstrate which rules of the Convention on the Continental Shelf may be considered, at least at this point, as expressing universal international law, and which rules are mere conventional provisions binding upon the parties to the Convention.

All instruments and proclamations concerning the continental shelf were unilateral acts of claiming states. Even the February 26, 1942, Treaty between Venezuela and the United Kingdom, by which each state recognized the claims of the other to parts of the Gulf of Paria, had the same effect on third states as a unilateral act, as it was *res inter alios acta* and thus not binding upon third states. Such acts could be analyzed in either of two ways. On the one hand, international law already recognized the rights of coastal states to the adjacent continental shelf, in which case the act was merely an assertion of an existing right. Alternatively, the question arises whether the existing law could be modified by a series of unilateral acts. Many shades of view have been voiced.

## The Continental Shelf as Part of the Customary Law?

As early as 1950, the authoritative voice of Professor H. Lauterpacht argued that the concept of the continental shelf was part of customary international law:

Four years in international relations is on the face of it too brief a period to make possible the creation of a new rule of customary law. However, assuming—an assumption which, it will be submitted, is unnecessary—that the emergence of the doctrine of sovereignty over the adjacent areas constituted a radical change in pre-existing international law, the length of time within which the customary rule of international law comes to fruition is irrelevant. For customary law is not yet another expression for prescription. A 'consistent and uniform usage practiced by States in question'—to use the language of the International Court of Justice in the *Asylum* case—can be packed within a short space of years. The 'evidence of a general practice as law'—in the words of Article thirty-eight of the Statute —need not be spread over decades. Any tendency to exact a prolonged period for the crystallization of custom must be in proportion to the degree and the intensity of the change that it purports, or is asserted, to effect. With regard to the submarine areas adjacent to the coast the assertion of sovereignty over them would constitute a drastic change in the law only if it could be shown that the international law of the sea—as distinguished from the deductions made by writers on the consequences of the principles of the freedom of the sea—actually prohibited, instead of being merely silent on the matter of the appropriation of the seabed and the subsoil outside the territorial waters. This, as will be submitted, is not the case. There is no significance in the circumstance that rights in submarine areas have been expressly asserted by some states only—by a minority of states. For it is apparent that most of the other states may have felt no need to put foward what, in the circumstances of the case, would be no more than a gesture.[8]

And continuing, Professor Lauterpacht concludes:

Unilateral declarations by traditionally law-abiding states, within a province which is particularly their own, when partaking of a pronounced degree of uniformity and frequency and when not followed by protests of other states, may properly be regarded as providing such proof of conformity with law as is both creative of custom and constituting evidence of it.[9]

Lauterpacht believed that the various claims to the continental shelf met a high degree of general acquiescence which was indicated by the absence of protests "except in isolated cases in which the proclamation of rights over the adjacent submarine areas been combined with, or has served as a cloak for, the assertion of claims to sovereignty over the high seas."[10] In Lauterpacht's opinion the International Law Commission, in laying down that the continental shelf was subject to the "sovereignty" of the coastal state, would merely be codifying existing practice:

The doctrine was that the continental shelf formed the prolongation of the territory of the coastal state in virtue of physical fact, and not by legal fiction. In cases where disputes concerning the continental shelf had been submitted to arbitration, it has been assumed without discussion that the consequence of proclamations by governments had been to give the coastal states full rights of sovereignty.[11]

---

[8] Lauterpacht, "Sovereignty over Submarine Areas," *Brit. Ybk. Int'l L.,* *1950*, vol. 27, pp. 393–94.

[9] *Ibid.* at 395.      [10] *Ibid.* at 393.

[11] Statement at a meeting of the International Law Commission, June 19, *1953*. *Ybk. Int'l L. Comm'n, 1953*, I, p. 86.

Another staunch advocate of the position that the concept of the continental shelf was recognized in customary international law was J. M. Yepes, delegate from Colombia. In answering the opposing arguments of Yuen-li Liang, a member of the United Nations Secretariat, Yepes suggested that:

[C]ustomary law [with respect to the continental shelf] did exist, although it did not respect traditional rules. Customary law was in the process of formation. Thus, the United Kingdom and Venezuela had shared the continental shelf between the mainland and the island of Trinidad. Thus, too, the Truman proclamation of 1945, the proclamations made by a number of Latin American States and by the Arab States in respect of sovereignty over continental shelves, had created international customary law. It was true that in the formation of that customary law on the continental shelf no account had been taken of *diuturnitas* which some publicists regarded as a necessary condition for the existence of customary law. But they were dealing with an exceptional case and *diuturnitas* was not absolutely essential provided they observed the principle of *opinio juris sive necessitatis*.[12]

It has been argued that customary international law may be formed by means of a series of unilateral claims if these claims are not protested, and Lauterpacht observed, as we noted, the limited nature of the protests against claims to the continental shelf. Although it is not certain whether dissenting states are obliged to express their disagreement by means of formal protest, it should be noted that states have not been entirely silent on the question of whether claims to the continental shelf are permitted by customary international law. In discussing a proposal of the International Law Commission, the Swedish government noted that:

The claims to control of the continental shelf and superjacent waters made after the Second World War must be considered as en-

---

[12] Meeting of June 26, 1953, *Ybk. Int'l L. Comm'n, 1953*, I. p. 122.

tirely new and, in the opinion of the Swedish Government, as having no foundation in existing international law. The Swedish Government was interested to note that in its comments on article 2 of the draft, the International Law Commission gives negative answers to the questions whether the continental shelf can be occupied and whether claims to sovereignty over it have any basis in international customary law. On the other hand, the Commission states that "the principle of the continental shelf is based upon general principles of law which serve the present-day needs of the international community." The Swedish Government is unable to reconcile these two views. Moreover, the Commission gives no particulars of the "general principles of law" to which it refers. The Swedish Government feels bound to regard any proposal to grant rights over the continental shelf to coastal States as being *de lege ferenda* and considers that such a proposal could only be put into effect by an international convention providing for certain concessions to coastal States which are in a position to exploit the continental shelf.[13]

Similar views were expressed by the governments of Israel,[14] Norway,[15] and the United Kingdom.[16]

Opposition to the view that claims to the continental shelf were recognized by customary international law was also voiced by Lord Asquith of Bishopstone, when acting as the umpire in the arbitral case of Petroleum Development (Trucial Coast) Limited *v.* The Ruler of Abu Dhabi. He there said that neither

---

[13] Comments by the Swedish Government, in Int'l L. Comm'n, *Report Covering the Work of the Fifth Session*, 8 U.N. *GAOR*, Supp. 9 (A/2456), p. 65, reprinted in *Ybk. Int'l L. Comm'n, 1953*, II, p. 263.

[14] *Ibid.*, at p. 59, *Ybk. Int'l L. Comm'n, 1953*, at p. 257. Israel "is of the opinion that that aspect of the law of the high seas which relates to the continental shelf is more susceptible to progressive development than to codification."

[15] *Ibid.*, at p. 63, *Ybk. Int'l L. Comm'n, 1953*, at p. 261. "[W]e are here faced not with a restatement or clarification of existing international law law but with the question of whether new rules should be established, . . ."

[16] *Ibid.*, at p. 68, *Ybk. Int'l L. Comm'n, 1953*, at p. 266: "State practice in regard to the subjects treated by the Commission has, notwithstanding certain gaps, been sufficiently developed to justify the attempts to prepare a code," but "some of the rules adumbrated by the Commission in its draft are not at present rules of customary international law."

the practice of nations nor the announcements of jurists give any certain and consistent answer to whether such claims were recognized by customary law, and that the continental shelf doctrine "cannot claim as yet to have assumed hitherto the hard lineaments of the definitive status of an established international law." After considering the wording of the draft articles and the accompanying comments of the International Law Commission, Lord Asquith observed that such articles are mere proposals *de lege ferenda*.[17]

The International Law Association also was opposed to treating the claims to the continental shelf as part of customary international law. Although an early report to the Association suggested the rule that:

control and jurisdiction over the seabed and subsoil of the continental shelf outside territorial waters can be vested in the coastal state by effective occupation, insofar as the continental shelf does not extend to the territorial waters of another state and is not shared with an adjacent state

was part of existing international law,[18] this report received strong opposition at the 1950 Copenhagen Conference and was withdrawn. By the 1952 Lucerne Conference, even more speakers opposed treating the claims as recognized by existing law [19] and little change was seen at the association's next conference in Edinburgh.[20]

---

[17] *International and Comparative Law Quarterly*, 1952, p. 247; [*1951*] *International Law Reports*, pp. 144–60, at 155.

[18] International Law Association, *Report of the Forty-Fourth Conference, Copenhagen, 1950*, pp. 133–35.

[19] See the views of Waldock, Gihl, Colban, Eustathiades, and Rygh expressed in International Law Association, *Report of the Forty-Fifth Conference, Lucerne, 1952*, p. 147–56.

[20] A majority of the relevant committee at the Edinburgh Conference were not prepared to say that any customary practice on the subject qualified it to be generally accepted as existing law. They noted the great variations in state claims and the protests lodged against the more extravagant of them. *Report of the Forty-Sixth Conference, Edinburgh, 1954*, p. 434.

Many writers, such as George Scelle, also argued against treating the continental shelf concept as customary international law. Their principal reasons were twofold—first, that unilateral acts, no matter how great in number, cannot create customary law, absence of protest being no proof of their general acceptance; second, that the principle of freedom of the seas prohibits individual states from claiming any part of the free sea, including the seabed and its subsoil. Many other writers, including Judge Manley O. Hudson,[21] Admiral M. W. Mouton,[22] and the present writer,[23] believed the doctrine of the continental

---

[21] Meeting of the Int'l L. Comm'n on June 6, 1950, *Ybk. Int'l Comm'n, 1950*, p. 5.

[22] "The Continental Shelf," *Recueil des Cours*, vol. 85, 1954, p. 435. See also Mouton, *The Continental Shelf*, 1952, p. 275; "We come to the provisional conclusion that the value of the unilateral acts is an initiative impulse to a new development in International Law. . . ."

[23] In a study on the continental shelf published in 1951, the author has expressed his view on the subject in the following manner: "When the continental shelf question came up, as a consequence of new economic factors, there were no special rules of international law recognizing any right of the coastal states to claim authority over the shelf. Therefore, the principle of the freedom of action belonging to every State was applied. This freedom is limited by factual circumstances, namely whether and to what extent a state may assure its rights against possible opposition from another state, and, furthermore, whether the step made by that state will be recognized by other states or will it be met with protests. All acts made up to the present [i.e., 1951] by different states have their legal basis in the principle mentioned above. This is the present-day [i.e, 1951] stage of development of the problem of the continental shelf. The proclamations made up to now are not sufficiently numerous and are not sufficiently widespread in all regions of the world, so they have not given rise to a new rule of customary international law. However, they constitute important precedents, especially because the states concerned have expressed their conviction that these steps are in conformity with international law. Moreover, at least the more moderate among these proclamations have met no formal protests from which circumstance one may infer that the conviction on the legality of these acts is becoming more widespread. Consequently, one may say that, as soon as a sufficient number of new similar proclamations appear, the moment will come when one may be justified in affirming that new rules concerning the continental shelf have been formed. This is because of the existence of a general conviction that every state has the right to claim a part of the continental shelf." (*Epikontinentalni pojas*, 1951, pp. 64–65.)

shelf to be nascent. In 1952 an intermediate position was expounded by Professor François. He thought that while coastal state "sovereignty" over the continental shelf was already *lex lata*, the details of the doctrine were only at the stage of *lex ferenda*.[24]

In 1956, the International Law Commission stated their view on the state of the law as follows:

The Commission does not deem necessary to expatiate on the question of the nature and legal basis of the sovereign rights attributed to the coastal state. The considerations relevant to this matter cannot be reduced to a single factor. In particular, it is not possible to base the sovereign rights of the coastal state exclusively on recent practice, for there is no question in the present case of giving the authority of a legal rule to a unilateral practice resting solely upon the will of the states concerned. However, that practice itself is considered by the Commission to be supported by considerations of law and of fact. In particular, once the seabed and the subsoil have become an object of active interest to coastal states with a view to the exploration and exploitation of their resources, they cannot be considered as *res nullius*, i.e., capable of being appropriated by the first occupier. It is natural that coastal states should resist any such solution. Moreover, in most cases the effective exploitation of natural resources must pre-suppose the existence of installations on the territory of the coastal state. Neither is it possible to disregard the geographical phenomenon whatever the term—propinquity, contiguity, geographical continuity, appurtenance or identity—used to define relationship between the submarine areas in question and the adjacent non-submerged land. All these considerations of general utility provide a sufficient basis for the principle of the sovereign rights of the coastal state as now formulated by the Commission. As

---

24 "Les réponses de quelques États font preuve d'une certaine hésitation au sujet de la question *lex lata* ou *lex ferenda*. A mon avis, il faudrait faire une distinction: *le principe* de la "souveraineté" de l'État côtier sur la plateau continental, tout en maintenant la liberté de la mer surjacente, pourrait être considéré déjà maintenant comme *lex lata* comme principe général de droit, mais toutes les questions de *détail* se trouvent encore dans la phase de *lex ferenda*." [Emphasis in original.] International Law Association, *Report of the Forty-Fifth Conference, Lucerne, 1952,* p. 145.

already stated, that principle, which is based on general principles corresponding to the present needs of the international community, is in no way incompatible with the principle of the freedom of the seas.[25]

## The Impact of the Geneva Convention

It is natural that opposition to recognition of the doctrine of the continental shelf as customary international law was strongest when the doctrine was first proclaimed. After the doctrine was included in the Convention on the Continental Shelf, writers were more prepared to consider it also as a customary rule. As one study noted:

Although it is a matter of opinion as to exactly when the parade of proclamations on the continental shelf developed a path which was not only discernible, but well defined and acknowledged, it seems clear and indisputable that the path has now been established; the practice of states in regard to the continental shelf has become a part of Customary International Law. The 1958 Geneva Convention on the Continental Shelf in effect was declaratory of this new customary international law: one may even say that the Convention codified the newly established law of the Continental Shelf.[26]

Since the 1958 Convention was signed, no serious objections have been voiced against the rule that every coastal state has ex-

---

[25] Int'l L. Comm'ns, *Report Covering the Work of its Eighth Session,* 11 U.N. *GAOR*, Supp. 9 (A/3159), pp. 42–43; *Ybk. Int'l L. Comm'n, 1956,* II, p. 298.

[26] Franklin, *supra* note 1, at p. 62. After the 1958 Convention Sørensen also recognized the claims being supported by customary international law. He observed that "claims concerning the subsoil and the seabed of the continental shelf were generally accepted, tacitly at least, by other states, and it is arguable that a customary rule of international law has developed on the basis of this practice." Sørensen, "The Law of the Sea," *International Conciliation,* 1958, No. 520, p. 227. Sørensen noted agreement by Waldock in "International Law and the New Maritime Claims," *International Relations,* April, 1956, at p. 187, and disagreement by Mouton, voiced in *The Continental Shelf,* 1952.

clusive rights over those areas designated by the Convention as part of the continental shelf. Thus, it is fair to conclude that this rule has been accepted as part of customary international law.

I would summarize the relationship of the doctrine of the continental shelf to customary international law as follows:

At the time of the first claims, no rule of customary international law recognized the right of coastal states to extend any form of authority over submarine areas outside their territorial sea. Rather, since the claimed area had, until that period, not been capable of being exploited, it was, from the legal point of view, nonexistent. It was in a position analogous to that of air space before the development of aviation, or outer space before rocket technology was developed. Therefore, it could not be considered either *res communis* or *res nullius*, since both concepts presuppose that the object in question be either reducible to possession or usable. Inaccessible objects or places cannot be subject to appropriation.

Thus, we must conclude that the newly claimed areas, because only recently accessible, were in a legal vacuum which should be filled with the aid of general principles.[27] One relevant principle of international law grants states freedom of action as long as such action is not specifically prohibited. Since they were not specifically prohibited, the first claims would be subsumed under this principle. These claims, which are precedents for a new practice, would become the basis of an established rule of law if sufficiently numerous and representative. An indication of their general acceptance is the fact that other states only protested against exaggerated claims.[28]

---

[27] See the recourse to the idea of legal *vacuum* suggested by François in the case of the pirate broadcasting off Netherlands' shores: van Panhuys & van Emde Boas, "Legal Aspects of Pirate Broadcasting," *Am. J. of Int'l L.,* 1966, pp. 315, 320.

[28] By the time these claims were asserted, activities along the continental shelf had already begun. Such activities needed regulation and this was most easily provided by the adjacent coastal state. Besides, that could effectively prevent other states from extending authority over the area in question. For these reasons, third states might not have voiced formal protests.

It has been argued that the importance of this absence of protest should not be overestimated because "protests have not been directed against the less exaggerated claims only because no state has had sufficient economic interest in the matter to challenge what might have been described as intention to commit a wrong." [29] However, since the doctrine of the continental shelf contains a challenge to the principle of freedom of the high seas —a fundamental principle for the last three centuries—the absence of protests gains meaning. Maritime powers are today, as they have been in the past, opposed to all attempts to encroach upon the freedom of the sea; they have formally protested such acts as extension of the territorial sea and the closing of bays and archipelagos. Besides, strong economic interests have found their legal expression in the principle of freedom of the seas. Therefore, the absence of protests against the more moderate claims cannot be considered as acquiescence. In its totality, however, this absence indicates a preparedness to accept a new trend which seems to be dictated by technical progress and economic needs. By 1958, this tendency became sufficiently strong to produce the development of a universally felt *opinio juris*.

In concluding we may say:

(1) The rule that every coastal state has exclusive rights over the area, as defined in the 1958 Geneva Convention as continental shelf, had been accepted without serious objection at the time of the signing of the convention. It can therefore be considered that this rule, set out in the convention, has also been accepted in customary international law.

(2) The same may be said of the rule that the exclusive right appertains to the coastal state *ipso jure*, without any declaration, proclamation, or effective exercise of this right. Consequently, no other state can intervene in this area or proclaim it, or part of it, as its own continental shelf.

(3) This right is somewhat less than sovereignty. Claims to

---

[29] O'Connell, "Sedentary Fisheries and the Australian Continental Shelf," *Am. J. Int'l L.*, 1955, p. 194.

sovereignty should be considered as contrary both to the convention and to customary international law.

These conclusions [30] were also arrived at by the International Court of Justice in its judgment in the *North Sea Continental Shelf Cases* of February 20, 1969. The Court shares the view that Articles 1, 2, and 3 of the Geneva Convention on the Continental Shelf are

the ones which, it is clear, were then regarded as reflecting, or as crystallizing, received or at least emergent rules of customary international law relative to the continental shelf, amongst them the question of the seaward extent of the shelf; the juridical character of the coastal State's entitlement; the nature of the rights exercisable; the kind of natural resources to which these relate; and the preservation intact of the legal status as high seas of the waters over the shelf, and of the superjacent air-space.[31]

We must, however, take exception with one of the points in the quoted judgment, namely, the inclusion of the provision concerning the seaward extent of the shelf among the "received" or "at least emergent rules of customary international law." With due respect for the dicta of the court, this author upholds another view, which is based upon the two following arguments: one relates to the seaward extent of the continental shelf (Article 1 of the Geneva Convention); the second relates to the delimitation of the continental shelf between two neighboring states (Article 6). Both points are discussed extensively in Chapters 6 and 7. There it is shown that the International Law Commission and the Geneva Conference itself had to choose between several possible solutions, none of them being considered as forming part of existing customary international law. On the contrary, the solutions laid down in the Convention on the Continental Shelf were arbitrarily chosen. With reference to the

---

[30] They were in the form as above written down in March, 1968.
[31] Judgment of February 20, 1969, *I.C.J. Reports, 1969*, p. 39.

equidistance rule in Article 6 of the convention, the International Court of Justice states that the International Law Commission

discussed various other possibilities as having equal if not superior status, such as delimitation by agreement, by reference to arbitration, by drawing lines perpendicular to the coast, by prolonging the dividing line of adjacent territorial waters . . . and on occasion the Commission seriously considered adopting one or other of these solutions.

The Court stated further that

at no time was the notion of equidistance as an inherent necessity of continental shelf doctrine entertained.[32]

This and other considerations led the Court to state:

In the light of these various considerations, the Court reaches the conclusion that the Geneva Convention did not embody or crystallize any pre-existent or emergent rule of customary law, according to which the delimitation of continental shelf areas between adjacent States must, unless the Parties otherwise agree, be carried out on an equidistance-special circumstances basis. A rule was of course embodied in Article 6 of the Convention, but as a purely conventional rule.[33]

The Court, after a thorough analysis of state practice, declared that Article 6 did not have the effect of constituting a rule of customary international law.[34]

The same conclusion should be drawn for that part of Article 1 which defines the outward limit of the continental shelf. It will be seen that the International Law Commission changed its views several times; shifting between the isobath limit and the exploitability test, and finally accepting both—not

---

[32] *Ibid.*, pp. 34, 35.    [33] *Ibid.*, p. 41.    [34] *Ibid.*, para. 81,

the happiest solution. With regard to the isobath limit, several depths were proposed both in the Commission and during the debates of the Geneva Conference itself. This fact demonstrates that the Commission and the Conference did not believe that there exists a customary rule for the outward limit of the continental shelf. The formula embodied in Article 1 was arbitrarily chosen and as such was not and did not become part of the customary international law.

Analogous situations regarding the relation between customary international law and conventional rules may be found elsewhere. For example, the Geneva Convention on the Territorial Sea adopts the old and generally accepted customary rule recognizing the sovereignty of coastal states over their territorial sea. The drafters of the Convention could not agree upon the breadth of the territorial sea, and there is no conventional rule concerning this point. If we consider that the question of the breadth of the territorial sea has not been settled in customary law, and if we suppose that the necessary majority at Geneva could have been found to accept a provision determining that breadth, such a provision could not be considered as accepted customary law, and would not be binding upon states which are not parties to the Convention.[35]

The writer's conclusions concerning the binding force of the rules of the 1958 Geneva Convention on the delimitation of the continental shelf have an important bearing on the problem

---

[35] As the Yugoslav delegate noted with regard to a similar problem: "Even if one of the proposals before the Conference were adopted by a two-thirds majority, and even if the corresponding convention were ratified by two-thirds of the States participating in the Conference, the breadth of the territorial sea would still not be fixed universally by international law. There was no provision of international law whereby a rule established by an agreement was binding on non-contracting States, so long as the juridical principle it expressed was not accepted, by reason of its universal application, as established juridical custom." (*Second United Nations Conference on the Law of the Sea, Official Records, Annexes and Final Act*, 1960, A/CONF.19/8, p. 133.)

we are discussing. The ultimate goal of preventing exaggerated claims to extended parts of submarine areas can be attained more easily if one is entitled to state that the provisions of the Convention concerning the outward limit of the continental shelf have no universal binding force, and that they must not be recognized by states which are not parties to the Convention. This legal situation also makes amendment of the present Convention easier.

# 5

## A Critical Examination of the Concept and Criteria of the Continental Shelf

~~~~~~~~~~~~~~~~~~~~~~~~~~~~~~~~~~~~~~~~~~~~~~~~~~~~~~~~~~~~~~~

SINCE THE CONVENTION ON THE CONTINENTAL SHELF CAME into force on June 10, 1964, there has been a constantly growing volume of discussion and criticism of its adequacy, in view of the rapid technological progress in the exploration of the ocean bed resources. The scale of this progress, which was not foreseen when the Convention was prepared, has caused a welter of new studies and proposals—by international organizations, national governments, academic institutions and scholars, and business organizations. These proposals will be surveyed in the concluding chapter. It is first necessary to examine the major implications of these new advances.

The principal problem—which is at the bottom of these many proposals and debates—is the claim now advanced from many quarters that as the now exploitable areas are part of the continental shelf they are subject to the exclusive control of some coastal state. In order to find a solution we must first consider four points: the relationship of the geological feature to the legal concept; [1] the significance of the 200-meter isobath limita-

---

[1] The fact that both concepts share the same name indicates some linkage. Besides, the existence of the geological feature was often used to justify claims of jurisdiction over submarine areas beyond the territorial sea.

tion; the significance of the exploitability test; and the significance of the adjacency test.

## Geological and Legal Concepts of the Continental Shelf

When states claim sovereignty or jurisdiction over portions of the continental shelf it is necessary to determine the extent of the claimed area. For reasons discussed below, the geological feature itself has not been used for fixing boundaries despite the fact that early claims were justified in terms of the scientific concept,[2] and the claimed areas, like the geological feature, were called "continental shelf." Instead, several claiming states defined the outer limits of their claims in terms of a particular isobath, an apparently simple method. In fact, even before 1945, the date when states first claimed authority over adjacent areas of the continental shelf, this method of defining the outer limits of the continental shelf had already been suggested. At the April 6, 1925, meeting of the Committee of Experts for the Progressive Codification of International Law, proposals were made to

draw up immediately, without regard to the extension or mainte-nance of maritime jurisdiction extending to the three mile limit, uni-form regulations for the exploitation of the industries of the sea, whose wealth constitutes a food reserve for humanity, over the whole extent of the ocean bed forming part of the continental shelf, i.e., the region along the coasts where the depth does not exceed 200 meters.[3]

The determination of the outer limits was one of the most serious problems facing the International Law Commission when it began working on a draft treaty concerning the continental shelf in 1949. The Commission believed the boundary of the geological feature to be an unsuitable guide because scientists

---

[2] See p. 50–51.    [3] *Am J. Int'l L.*, Special Number, July, 1926, p. 231.

were not in agreement on the definition of the continental shelf. As François, the rapporteur of the Commission noted, "[t]he varied use of the term by scientists is in itself an obstacle to the adoption of the geological concept as a basis for legal regulation of the problem." [4] Besides, as both François and George Scelle, the Commission Chairman, noted, no member of the Commission could advocate a linking of special rights to the presence of a continental shelf. Rather, all littoral states, whether or not they possessed continental shelves, should enjoy the same rights.[5]

The Commission decided to formulate a legal concept of the continenal shelf which is not linked with the geological approach. It conceived the legal concept as a means of encouraging the exploitation of the natural resources of the seabed and subsoil, a function not connected to the origin or form of the geological feature.

On the other hand, various members of the Commission did want the legal concept to approximate the geological. In the opinion of F. I. Kojevnikov, the definition of the continental

---

[4] Int'l L. Comm'n, *Report Covering the Work of its Third Session*, 6 U.N. *GAOR*, Supp. 9 (A/1858), p. 17, reprinted at *Ybk. Int'l L. Comm'n, 1951*, II, p. 141.

[5] Manley Hudson proposed that "[c]ontrol and jurisdiction over the sea-bed and subsoil of submarine areas outside the marginal sea may be exercised by a littoral State for the exploration and exploitation of the natural resources therein contained, to the extent to which such exploitation is feasible." He explained that his avoidance of the term "continental shelf," and his use of the "possibility of exploitation" test, permitted states which, in the opinion of many authors, are without any continental shelf—having no slope toward greater depths, such as those bordering the Persian Gulf—to make claims. However, as Spiropoulos observed, Hudson's formula might permit a state to extend its control to the middle of the ocean. Thereupon Hudson suggested limiting a littoral state's rights to areas located on the continental shelf, "including regions which may be assimilated to the continental shelf by reason of the shallowness of their waters," and therefore connected with the claiming state's territory. The Commission refused to adopt his approach. Instead it approved Brierly's proposal that "the area for such control and jurisdiction will need definition but it need not depend on the existence of a continental shelf." *Ybk. Int'l L. Comm'n, 1950*, I, pp. 218-23. Such Commission action indicated a desire not to link the legal concept of the continental shelf with the geological approach.

shelf required a more solid basis which apparently was to be found in the natural geographic factors. Kojevnikov proposed that "[a]s here used, the term continental shelf means the seabed and subsoil of the submarine areas contiguous to the coast, but lying outside of the area of the territorial waters, up to the line *where the steep slope of the seabed begins.*" [6] (Emphasis added.) Another objection was voiced by Faris Bey el Khoury who believed that defining the continental shelf by depth was impracticable since, given the configuration of the seabed, its boundaries would be as highly indented as the coasts of Norway and Greece.[7]

After deliberation, the commission adopted the exploitability test. Article 1 of the first draft of the proposed Convention, adopted in 1951, states:

As here used, the term "continental shelf" refers to the seabed and subsoil of the submarine areas contiguous to the coast, but outside the areas of territorial waters, where the depth of the superjacent waters admits of the exploitation of the natural resources of the seabed and subsoil.[8]

This draft was immediately criticized by both governments and scholars for being too vague, and permissive of unlimited expansion.[9] As an alternative, the governments of France, Iceland,[10] South Africa, the United Kingdom, and Yugoslavia, and

---

[6] Meeting of June 17, 1953. *Ybk. Int'l L. Comm'n, 1953*, I, p. 74.

[7] *Ibid.*, p. 75.

[8] Int'l L. Comm'n, *supra* note 4, Supp. 9 (A/1858), at 17, *Ybk. Int'l L. Comm'n, 1951*, II, at 141.

[9] As Mouton noted, "when does this possibility exist? When a new device comes off the drawing desk of a drilling engineer?" François, *Fourth Report on The Regime of the High Seas* (the *Continental Shelf and Related Subjects*), A/CN.4/60, p. 24, reprinted at *Ybk. Int'l L. Comm'n, 1953*, II, p. 9. Another aspect of this criticism involves an installation which after being operated for a period of time proves to be a failure. Since exploitation was impossible, the installation, having perhaps hampered navigation, and its authorization were "illegal." *Ibid.*

[10] Subject to investigation as to whether the 100-fathom isobath was an appropriate limit.

such scholars as V. Brajkovié, C. F. Driessen, G. Gidel, M. W. Mouton, and C. H. M. Waldock suggested that the outer limits of the continental shelf be defined in terms of the 100-fathom 200-meter isobath.

By 1953, both the Commission and its rapporteur had changed their minds. As the latter noted, although there is force in the arguments in favor of an exploitation test, it is "wiser to accept at least a provisional limit, which might be re-examined if technical development so required." In justifying his reversal of position, he stressed that the exploitation test might create considerable problems by allowing the exclusive rights of coastal states to be extended to unlimited depths and unlimited distances from the coast.[11] The Commission redrafted Article 1 to state "[a]s used in these articles, the term "continental shelf" refers to the seabed and subsoil of the submarine areas contiguous to the coast, but outside the area of the territorial sea, *to a depth of two hundred meters*." (Emphasis added.) [12] It explained the change in the following comments to the new draft:

The text previously adopted does not satisfy the requirement of certainty and . . . it is calculated to give rise to disputes. On the other hand, the limit of 200 meters—a limit which is *at present* sufficient for all practical needs—has been fixed because it is at that depth that the continental shelf, in the geological sense, generally comes to an end. It is there that the continental slope begins and falls deeply to a great depth. The text thus adopted is not wholly arbitrary for, as already stated, it takes into account the practical possibilities, *so far as they can be foreseen at present*, of exploration and exploitation. [Emphasis added.] [13]

The Commission further noted that their solution would include shallow submarine areas lacking a continental slope, such

[11] Francois, *supra* note 9, A/CN.4/60, at 102, *Ybk. Int'l L. Comm'n, 1953*, II, at 38.

[12] Int'l L. Comm'n, *Report Covering the Work of its Fifth Session*, 8 U.N. *GAOR* Supp. 9 (A/2456), p. 12, reprinted *Ybk. Int'l L. Comm'n, 1953*, II, p. 212.

[13] *Ibid.* at 213.

as the Persian Gulf, despite the fact that they are not considered part of the continental shelf as that term is "generally understood." [14]

In 1956 the Commission again changed its mind. After reconsidering the definition of the continental shelf it

noted that the Inter-American Specialized Conference on "Conservation of Natural Resources: Continental Shelf and Oceanic Waters, held at Ciudad Trujillo (Dominican Republic) [known now as Santo Domingo], in March 1956, had arrived at the conclusion that the right of the coastal State should be extended beyond the limit of 200 meters, "to where the depth of superjacent waters admits of the exploitation of the natural resources of the seabed and subsoil." Certain members thought that the Article adopted in 1953 should be modified. While agreeing that in present circumstances the limit adopted is in keeping with practical needs, they disapproved of a provision prohibiting exploitation of the continental shelf at a depth greater than 200 meters, even if such exploitation was a practical possibility. They thought that in the latter case, the right to exploit should not be made subject to prior alteration of the limit adopted. While maintaining the limit of 200 meters in this article as the normal limit corresponding to present needs, they wished to recognize forthwith the right to exceed that limit if exploitation of the seabed or subsoil at a depth greater than 200 meters proved technically possible. It was therefore proposed that the following words should be added to the Article, "or beyond that limit to where the depth of the superjacent waters admits of the exploitation of the natural resources of the said areas." In the opinion of certain members this addition would also have the advantage of not encouraging the belief that up to 200 meters depth there is a fixed zone where rights of sovereignty other than those stated in Article 68 below can be exercised. Other members contested the usefulness of the addition, which in their opinion unjustifiably and dangerously impaired the stability of the limit adopted. The majority of the Commission nevertheless decided in favour of the addition. [15]

---

14 *Ibid.* at 213–14.

15 Int'l L. Comm'n, *Report Covering the Work of its Eighth Session,* U.N. *GAOR* Supp. 9 (A/3159), p. 41, reprinted *Ybk. Int'l L. Comm'n, 1956,* II, p. 296–97. Article 68 became Article 2 of the Convention.

This formula, as adopted by the Commission in 1956, was incorporated into the 1958 Geneva Convention on the Continental Shelf and is now in force.

## Five Possible Criteria of Delimitation

Let us now consider five criteria which could be taken as bases for delimitation: (1) the outer limits of the shelf as defined for geological purposes; (2) a predetermined distance from the coast; (3) a predetermined depth or isobath; (4) an exploitability test; (5) an adjacency test.

(1) Although the boundary of the geological feature might appear to be the most appropriate boundary for the legal concept, no serious attempt has been made to use it [16] since it has never been clearly defined. Steep falling off may occur at various depths and at various distances from the shore. Besides, irregularity of gradients makes it difficult to ascertain when it occurs. Thus, the natural phenomenon is in itself an uncertain basis for delimitation purposes.

(2) Limitations can be expressed in terms of a predetermined distance from the coastline. This method must be seriously considered since it provides a reasonably equitable, as well as clearly determinable and easily applicable, criterion. It would benefit coastal states surrounded by sharp drop-offs near the shore. In fact, several Latin American states, finding themselves surrounded by rather narrow shelves, and therefore at a great disadvantage from the geological point of view, used this method to claim rights extending 200 miles from the coast. These claims, though, were protested.[17] Use of this method was

---

[16] But see Kojevnikov's proposal, Meeting of June, 17, 1953, *Ybk. Int'l L. Comm'n, 1953*, I, p. 74, and the Brierly proposal that the exclusive right of exploitation of the continental shelf cannot extend beyond the limit of the continental shelf. Brierly's proposal was immediately opposed and was never pursued. Meeting of July 13, 1950, *Ybk. Int'l L. Comm'n, 1950*, I, p. 224.

[17] See pp. 42–45.

also proposed in 1950 by the rapporteur of the International Law Commission. After observing that isobath limitations would give states unequal portions of the seabed, thus causing "unjustifiable inequality," he requested that the governments express themselves either for a limit based upon specific distance from the coast or upon depth.[18]

(3) Another method of fixing the outer limit of the area, and one often used, is to do so in terms of the depth of the superjacent water. President Truman utilized this method when proclaiming the first claim to the continental shelf. It was subsequently used by most other states, and it was finally codified by the 1958 Geneva Convention on the Continental Shelf.

While ease of applicability might initially appear to be a virtue of this method, since a particular state's claim is clearly terminated at the point where the superjacent water level first exceeds a predetermined depth, it is in fact difficult to precisely ascertain where this spot occurs because of the many irregularities of the ocean floor.

A further disadvantage of the isobath limit approach is the inequality that results from the diverse size of the claims of the various coastal states which, in turn, depend upon the size of shallow waters. Of course, this method would not afford states a practical advantage as long as the natural resources within their zone of control were located at a depth too deep to exploit. Despite these drawbacks, limitation in terms of a predetermined isobath is probably the best method, as evidenced by its general adoption in unilateral acts and in the codification work that led to the 1958 Convention.

(4) Use of the criterion or test of exploitability is understandable when it is necessary to delimit the rights of coastal states with respect to the exploitation of natural resources. This was first considered during the period when the International

---

[18] François, "Report on the High Seas," 1950, A/CN.4/17, at 39–40, reprinted *Ybk. Int'l L. Comm'n 1950*, II, at 51.

Law Commission was preparing a draft convention on the continental shelf. This test was finally adopted, after a period of disfavor, as a complementary test used to define the scope of the continental shelf.[19]

It remains to examine the meaning of "exploitability" for purposes of Article 1 of the Convention. To analyze this question, we must distinguish between availability, accessibility, sufficiency of technology to undertake exploitation, and profitability. Availability refers to the actual existence of particular natural resources in the claimed area. Even when these resources exist, they do not become accessible to man until technological advances permit exploration and, possibly, the gathering of a few samples. The ability to undertake such activities, though, does not mean that bulk recovery is possible. Of course, if the existence of the resources is known, and a need for them exists, a technique for recovery can be perfected. However, even such progress does not ensure that bulk recovery will occur. Large-scale mining will only occur if costs are sufficiently low, or the resources sufficiently needed to yield the entrepreneur a profit.

Exploitability depends upon the type of technique used. For example, gravel dredging may be possible at greater depths than oil drilling, or vice versa, whereas harvesting sedentary living organisms may be possible at still greater depths.[20] Thus, another problem in interpreting the exploitability test is to decide which technique is determinative. An important variation of this problem is the question of which state must control the technology that makes exploitation possible, and in what geographical area must such exploitation be possible.

---

[19] Henkin, *Law for the Sea's Mineral Resources*, 1968, p. 42, considers the definition in Article 1 of the Continental Shelf Convention outdated. The rapid advances in technology are rendering its exploitability clause meaningless as a definition of the outer limit of the shelf.

[20] "Petroleum could be sought at a shallow depth—30 meters—precious metals could perhaps be sought at lower levels—60 to 70 meters." François, at Meeting of June 18, 1953, *Ybk. Int'l L. Comm'n, 1953*, I, p. 79.

There are three possible solutions. One would require the claiming state itself to have sufficient technology to exploit the resources of the claimed area. Another would only require that somebody be able to exploit the resources of the claimed area. This solution is predicated on the idea that if adequate technology exists, the claiming state could license or hire any enterprise controlling it to undertake the exploitation so that needed resources would not be wasted. Its requirements, though, would not be fulfilled when exploitation at a particular depth was undertaken in an area other than the one claimed, since such climatic and oceanographic factors as the strength of currents, winds, waves, and the solidity of the ocean floor might not permit exploitation at a comparable depth in the area in question. The third would require only that exploitation at a given depth be possible somewhere in the world. This solution might call for

. . . each party to file periodically with the Secretary-General of the United Nations a statement indicating the maximum depth at which it is exploiting the resources of its shelf. The greatest such figure, established to the satisfaction of the Secretary-General, would determine the shelf limits for all parties until the next succeeding report.[21]

The answer to this problem is quite important to the less-developed countries. As the Jamaican delegate to the United Nations observed:

The third point of urgency that I should like to mention relates to the fact that today only a few countries possess the technological and scientific capability for exploring the seabed and subsoil thereof. Indeed, only a few countries are today able to compete effectively for the fisheries of the seas. Consequently, the smaller and poorer countries are at a disadvantage. It should be sheer economic shortsightedness and chaos if such countries should in time find them-

---

[21] Young, "The Geneva Convention of the Continental Shelf: A First Impression," *Am. J. Int'l L.,* 1958, p. 733, at 735–36.

selves locked out of possibilities for future exploration. That seems to be the situation concerning fishing rights in "historic fishing grounds." It is submitted, in the spirit of the United Nations Charter, that these developing countries should be able to share in the resources as the common property of the world community. Unless that was done, then it might be predicted, based on past experience, that the advanced countries, having asserted their rights and claims to these areas, should not be disposed to yield to newcomers.[22]

In recognition of such potential deprivation of the less-developed countries, Arthur H. Dean stated that although "[t]he language [of Article 1] is susceptible of at least two interpretations: (1) that the outer boundaries of the shelf are dependent upon the actual technological ability of the particular nation concerned, and (2) that boundaries are determined by the technological ability of the most advanced nation." Dean rejected the first interpretation and explained: "The convention was predicated on the notion that each nation, whether technologically advanced or not, has sovereign rights over its portion of the continental shelf. The convention explicitly provides that its rights are not diminished by failure to exploit; . . ."[23]

---

[22] General Assembly, First Committee, November 15, 1967, A/C.1/PV. 1529.

[23] Dean, "The Law of the Sea Conference, 1958–60, and Its Aftermath," in Alexander (ed.), *The Law of the Sea*, 1967, p. 247. Discussion of this problem has been summarized as follows: "Several alternatives were suggested concerning the status of the seabed beyond the limits of the continental shelf. One was that any development of minerals of the seabed or subsoil beyond the shelf might be seen as justifying an extension of the shelf itself, with no limit placed on the depths involved. But would the extension of one country's capabilities (and control) to depths, say, of 600 meters, imply that all other coastal countries also lay claim to the seabed of their own coasts to an equal depth? If actual exploitation becomes a criteria for claims beyond the 200 meter isobath, would this not favor the technically advanced countries to the detriment of other coastal states? Or would it turn out that any country which has exploitable resources on or beneath the seabed off its coasts might permit exploitation of these resources by one of the technically advanced countries and thus would be able to claim the seabed out to and including the site of these resources as its own?" *Ibid.*, pp. 186–87.

It seems unnecessary to require particular states, or the nationals thereof, to possess technical expertise, since that can be obtained by anybody possessing sufficient capital or by those states which grant exploitation concessions to expert companies. It should be added, however, that exploitation must actually be possible in the area claimed. The mere fact that exploitation has been undertaken in one area at a depth of 150 meters, for example, is no proof that such exploitation is possible in another area of the same depth. Thus, if anybody wishes to explore or exploit natural resources near the coast of State A, that person must obtain a permit from State A. If conditions do not permit exploitation there, State A would not be able to continue licensing operations. On the other hand, if operations have been undertaken before permission is granted and exploitation is possible, State A could require the would-be exploiter to discontinue his activities.

(5) Still another possible criterion is "adjacency," which is also included in Article 1 of the Convention on the Continental Shelf, and expressed in this article by the words "submarine areas adjacent to the coast." Justification for its use stems from the fact that all state's rights over areas of the sea are derived from the exercise by the state of its dominion over the corresponding coast. Thus, if a state loses control over the coast, it would lose its control over the internal waters, the territorial sea, and the continental shelf. As the Permanent Court of Arbitration noted in the boundary case between Sweden and Norway, concerning Grisbadarna,

Whereas, Norway has held the contention, which for that matter has not been rejected by Sweden, that from the sole fact of the Peace of Roskilde in 1658 the maritime territory in question was divided automatically between her and Sweden; whereas, the Tribunal fully endorses this opinion; whereas, this opinion is in conformity with the fundamental principles of the law of nations, both ancient and modern, in accordance with which *the maritime territory is an essential appurtenance of land territory*, whence it follows that at the time when, in 1658, the land territory called the Bohuslan was ceded to Sweden, the radius of maritime territory constituting an inseparable appurtenance of this land territory must have automatically formed a part of this cession.[24] [Emphasis added.]

Similarly, in the *Anglo-Norwegian Fisheries Case* of 1951, the International Court of Justice noted that "among these considerations, some reference must be made to the close dependence of the territorial sea upon the land domain. *It is the land which confers upon the coastal State a right to the waves off its coasts.*" [25] [Emphasis added.]

In his recent study on the law for the sea's mineral resources, Louis Henkin rejects the exploitability test and the "liaison" with the geological shelf concept. He characterizes the extreme interpretation of the continental shelf definition in Article 1 as a colossal "grabbing" by coastal states.[26] In his opinion

interpretation must find an outer limit to the legal shelf not in the 200 meter isobath or in the exploitability clause, but in the phrase "submarine areas adjacent to the coast," read in the context, and spirit, of the history of the Convention.[27]

## *The Meaning of "Exploitability" under Article 1 of the Geneva Convention*

The crucial question, however, concerning the exploitability criterion in Article 1 of the Convention on the Continental Shelf is the following: To what extent does the definition in Article 1 permit the extension of the claims of coastal states to-

---

[24] *The Grisbadarna Case,* October 23, 1909. Scott, *Hague Court Reports,* 1916, p. 127.

[25] *I.C.J. Reports, 1951,* p. 133. See, also *The North Sea Continental Shelf Cases, I.C.J. Reports, 1969,* pp. 22, 29: "the right of the coastal State is based on its sovereignty over the land domain."

[26] Henkin, *supra,* note 19, at 18–19.

[27] *Ibid.,* p. 21. See also McDougal & Burke, *The Public Order of the Oceans,* 1962, p. 688: "continuity and proximity are prerequisites to coastal control."

wards the submarine areas of the high seas when technological progress will make the exploitation of natural resources at great depths possible? The language of the Article is subject to several possible interpretations. An extreme approach, resting solely on the exploitability test, would permit all submarine areas to be claimed someday by coastal states. Of course, this result would not be immediately effected. Since technology will only advance in stages, claims to exclusive rights over greater depths will also advance gradually. However such a process will serve to further acceptance of this interpretation. Besides, those governments and scholars which favor the complete partitioning of all submarine areas might well argue that this solution is the only one which can provide a precise answer to the meaning of "exploitability," thus permitting planning.

On the other hand, such total apportionment of the ocean floor would, as we shall see in the next chapter, result in great inequities. Moreover, as our past experiences in granting sovereignty over relatively restricted areas of the continental shelf have shown, it would also affect conditions on the surface of the sea. For these reasons, an expansive interpretation of Article 1 is undesirable, and was not envisioned by the framers of the Convention. The legislative history shows that they wished to establish a relationship between the isobath limit and the exploitability test, and that they wished to use the adjacency test.

Neither the members of the International Law Commission, nor the delegates to the 1958 Geneva Conference regarded the exploitability test as an independent criterion for determining the outer limits of the continental shelf. The test was first introduced in order to avoid the disadvantages inherent in fixing the boundaries of the legal concept in terms of the geological feature or a predetermined isobath.[28] Later, when the 200-meter iso-

---

[28] See the discussion earlier in this chapter, and Chapter 7, on the disadvantages of these methods and the reason why the exploitability test was used.

bath was adopted as the outer boundary of the continental shelf, the exploitability test was added so that coastal states surrounded by an otherwise narrow continental shelf might someday be able to claim larger areas.

Of course, the framers of the Convention were aware that the exploitability test would create some measure of elasticity. However, while this consequence was mentioned many times in the various debates on the definition of the continental shelf, no record of the proceedings of either the International Law Commission or the Geneva Conference indicates that Article 1 could or should be interpreted as requiring the eventual subdivision of the entire ocean floor. One possible explanation of this lack of foresight is that maritime technology in the fifties was quite backward compared to the progress attained by the mid-sixties. Oil drilling, the most important means of exploitation during the period preceding the Conference, was not then feasible beyond a depth of 280 feet; [29] projects to develop methods of drilling in deeper waters had not yet begun; and bathyscaphes, Sealab, and submersibles of the Alvin and Deepstar type were in their infancy. Thus, although scientific and technological circles might have foreseen exploitation in deeper waters, general opinion was not aware of the possibility.

To be sure, the International Law Commission and the delegates to the 1958 Geneva Conference were aware of isolated warnings that future exploitation might be possible at depths

---

[29] At the Meeting on August 7, 1953, of the International Law Commission, the rapporteur observed that "cases where exploitability extends beyond a depth of two hundred metres" did not at present exist. The present limit of exploitability was usually no greater than 30 meters, and the presently foreseeable limit is no greater than 60 or 70 meters. He therefore thought that the commission had been extremely generous in setting the limit at 200 meters, although he admitted that if exploitability was ever possible at depths beyond 200 meters the commission's limit would become arbitrary, but he thought it went without saying that the definition which the commission had adopted was designed to meet present and *foreseeable* needs. *Ybk. Int'l L. Comm'n, 1953,* I, p. 338.

greater than 200 meters so that the exploitability test would permit excessive claims. For example, in their comments on the draft, the Chilean and South African governments drew attention to the fact that with the advance of technical efficiency, the boundaries of the continental shelf would be subject to continual revision.[30] The International Law Commission also showed an appreciation of future technological progress. In their commentary to their 1951 draft of Article 1 they stated that "technical developments in the near future might make it possible to exploit resources of the seabed at a depth over two hundred meters." [31]

However, most of the delegates at Geneva apparently did not believe that technological advances would be rapid enough to make the exploitability test a lever of constantly expanding claims. One expert, Mouton, wrote an influential preparatory paper for the Conference in which he states that he did not believe exploitation at great depths to be possible for at least twenty years.[32]

---

[30] François, *supra* note 9, A/CN.4/60, at 17, 20–21, *Ybk. Int'l L. Comm'n, 1953*, II, at 6, 7–8. This observation was later supported by the German delegate to the 1958 Geneva Conference who predicted that future exploitations would be possible at depths of 600–800 or even 1,000 meters. U.N. Conference on the Law of the Sea, Official Records, vol. 6 (A/CONF. 13/42), p. 37–38.

[31] Int'l L. Comm'n, *supra* note 4, Supp 9 (A/1858), at 18, *Ybk. Int'l L. Comm'n, 1951*, II, p. 141. Gidel and Driessen also criticized the exploitability test. Driessen, in particular, warned of how such tests could lead to excessive claims. See François, *supra* note 9, A/CN.4/60, at 21–22, 23, *Ybk. Int'l L. Comm'n, 1953*, II, at 8.

[32] In a paper prepared for the 1958 Geneva Conference, Mouton noted that during 1956 and 1957 fixed oil platforms were installed in the Gulf of Mexico in waters 112 and 120 feet deep (36.6 meters). A mobile unit, designed to operate at depths of 150 feet (45.7 meters), had been used. A Texas Tower had been installed in the Atlantic Ocean in waters more than 180 feet deep (55 meters). He also observed that drilling from floating vessels had been accomplished at depths of 275 feet (83.8 meters); tin ore bucket dredgers regularly operated in 30–35 meters of water, and a ship dredging tin off Thailand had operated at depths of 215–220 feet (65.5–67.1 meters). Mouton believed that depths of 200 feet (61 meters) were the maximum at which the then existing oil drilling platforms could be used. And he did not foresee the possibility of the oil industry developing structures permitting drilling at 400 feet (122 meters) in less than ten years, and at 200

A different approach was taken by the United States delegate to the Conference, Miss Marjorie Whiteman.

[S]he doubted whether, in an age of rapid scientific progress, it would be wise to limit the area of exploitation [by means of an isobath limit]. Only a few years previously exploitation of the seabed and subsoil in 200 meters of water had seemed the maximum achievable, but scientists were already talking in terms of a much higher order of magnitude. Exploitation could not, however, continue indefinitely towards the middle of the ocean; the continental slope fell away steeply and rapidly, so that exploitation beyond a certain limit would not be an economic proposition.[33]

Besides, many of the delegates who were aware of the effect of future technological advances on the exploitability test concentrated their efforts on revising the 200-meter isobath limitation to what they considered a more reasonable level. For example, India proposed an increase to 1,000 meters "so as to cover future eventualities." [34] While such efforts were abandoned because the 200-meter limit seemed presently sufficient, it was understood that when technological advances rendered such limit obsolete a new conference would be convened to revise it. These efforts reinforce the author's conclusion that the framers of the Convention did not intend the exploitability test to be used to permit a limitless extension of the continental shelf.[35]

---

meters in less than 20 years. Mouton, "Recent Developments in the Technology of Exploiting the Mineral Resources of the Continental Shelf," A/CONF.13/25. In the preparatory stages Mouton had argued against the exploitability test because there was little likelihood of exploitation at depths greater than 200 meters. François, *supra* note 9, A/CN.4/60, p. 24, *Ybk. Int'l L. Comm'n*, II, p. 9.

[33] *1958 Conference on the Sea*, vol. 6 (A/CONF.13/42), p. 40.

[34] *Ibid.*, p. 42.

[35] In fact, advocates of proposals to increase the isobath limitation must have considered that the test was the dominant element of the definition. If they believed that the exploitability test would sufficiently provide for increasing exploitation possibilities they would not have attempted to change the isobath limits.

Furthermore, the exploitability criterion should not be taken as being isolated, but rather as connected with other elements of the definition. The framers of the convention intended that the exploitability test only supplement the 200-meter isobath test in exceptional circumstances; in normal times they considered the isobath test controlling. They indicated this by appending the exploitability test to the isobath limitation by the words "or beyond that limit." Moreover, if the exploitabilty test were applicable whenever areas lying beyond the 200-meter isobath were exploitable, the isobath limitation would be rendered nugatory.

Since the principles of legal construction require that whenever possible meaning be attributed to all elements of a definition, this view of the exploitability test is improper.[36] Although for reasons of legal technique the definition contained in Article 1 could not be based upon the geological definition, the close relationship [37] between the two indicates that the scientific concept bears upon the interpretation of the legal concept. Article 1 could therefore be interpreted as limiting coastal state authority to those submarine areas that geologists would consider continental shelves and which, unless exceptional reasons exist, are covered by water less than 200 meters deep.

The adjacency test, the third element in the Article 1 definition, provides another argument against an overly expansive interpretation of the exploitability test. As the French govern-

---

[36] Similar reasoning can be applied to "adjacency" test, discussed below.

[37] This relationship is indicated by four factors: the identity of names, the fact that early claims to areas of the continental shelf were justified as being claims to submerged and inseparable parts of the coastal land mass, the fact that initial efforts at codifying the law relating to submarine areas attempted to define those areas in terms of the geological notion of the continental shelf, and the fact that the legal concept has been defined, *inter alia*, in terms of the 200-meter isobath, the average outer limit of the geological feature. It may be recalled that at the time of the first claims, the natural continental shelf was claimed, among other reasons, on the assumption that it was, during an earlier geological period, dry land.

ment properly noted when depositing their accession to the Convention, "the expression 'adjacent' areas implies a notion of geophysical, geological and geographical dependence which *ipso facto* rules out an unlimited extension of the continental shelf." [38] While British and American communications concerning France's declaration are reserved, they do not reject France's interpretation.[39] Thus, the adjacency test indicates that for purposes of the Convention the continental shelf only includes those areas having a geophysical, geological, and geographical link with some coastal land mass, and does not include the remainder of the seabed. It should also cover such cases where one country's coast is separated from a wide continental shelf by a narrow deep near to the shore. In this connection, the members of the Commission had the case of Norway especially in mind, as explained in the following comment of the Commission:

In the special cases in which submerged areas of a depth less than 200 meters, situated fairly close to the coast, are separated from the part of the continental shelf adjacent to the coast by a narrow channel deeper than 200 meters, such shallow areas could be considered as adjacent to that part of the shelf. It would be for the State relying on this exception to the general rule to establish its claim to an equitable modification of the rule.[40]

Such exception is necessary to avoid the otherwise undesirable consequences that would arise in situations like the Norwegian

---

[38] *United Nations Treaty Series*, vol. 538, p. 336.

[39] The Government of the United Kingdom declared that they "take note of the declaration of the Government of the French Republic and reserve their position concerning it." The Government of the United States stated that "declarations made by France with respect to Article 1 and Article 2 are noted without prejudice." *United Nations Treaty Series*, Vol. 551, p. 334, and Vol. 544, p. 377.

[40] Int'l L. Comm'n, *supra* note 13, Supp. 9 (A/3159), at 42, *Ybk. Int'l L. Comm'n, 1956*, II, at 297. See also, *Ibid.*, at 43, *Ybk. Int'l L. Comm'n, 1956*, II, at 298: "Neither is it possible to disregard the geographical phenomenon whatever the term—propinquity, contiguity, geographical continuity, appurtenance or identity—used to define the relationship between the submarine areas in question and the adjacent non-submerged land."

Trough. If that exception did not exist, Great Britain could claim all the area from its coast to the Norwegian Trough since that trough is the first fall-off from the British coast, and the water level between Britain, and it is shallow. However, when technology reached a state at which the lowest point in the Trough could be exploited, Norway, too, would claim at least some of the area between the Trough and Britain. The area thus belonging to Norway could only be limited by the application of the provisions of Article 6 of the Convention on the Continental Shelf. Then the part of the initially British continental shelf would become Norwegian, as a consequence of increased exploitability.[41]

In the *North Sea Continental Shelf Cases,* the International Court of Justice used the adjacency test as an argument against an overall application of the equidistance rule. The Court observed that adjacency is not always identical with proximity. This means that a part of the continental shelf may sometimes be considered as adjacent to State A, although it is nearer to the coast of State B.[42] The Court linked the notion of adjacency to a "more fundamental" principle of the natural prolongation or continuation of the land territory into and under the high seas. The same argument must also be used with respect to the question of the seaward extent of the continental shelf. Claims to the continental shelf must remain within the limits dictated by the natural link between the land domain and claimed submarine areas.

To summarize, while a literal reading of the exploitability test would permit individual coastal states to extend their sovereign rights to submarine areas in the middle of the ocean, such a possibility was not intended by the framers of the Convention, and it would ignore the relationship of the exploitability test to

---

[41] The United Kingdom and Norway signed an Agreement on delimitation on March 3, 1964, using the median line between the shores of both countries as the boundary. They thus ignored the existence of the Norwegian Trough.

[42] *I.C.J. Reports, 1969,* p. 30.

the 200-meter isobath test and the adjacency test. Unfortunately, although the above interpretation is improper, the precise limits of the continental shelf and the appropriate circumstances for applying the exploitability test are unknown, and the adjacency test has never been clearly explained. Until these uncertainties are settled, and an interpretation offering definite boundaries proposed, there is a risk that man's need for precision will encourage him to accept the literal reading of the exploitability test as authoritative. The best way to avoid this possibility would be to redraft Article 1.

# 6

## The Delimitation of the Continental Shelf
## in Special Circumstances

~~~~~~~~~~~~~~~~~~~~~~~~~~~~~~~~~~~~~~~~~~~~~~~~~

### *Division of the Continental Shelf*
### *Between Neighboring States*

Article 6 of the Convention on the Continental Shelf deals
with the problem of how the continental shelf should be divided
among neighboring states. In this chapter we shall consider the
proffered solutions and how they relate to an interpretation of
Article 1 of the Convention. Article 6 states that:

1. Where the same continental shelf is adjacent to the territories of
two or more States whose coasts are opposite each other, the boundary of the continental shelf appertaining to such States shall be determined by agreement between them. In the absence of agreement,
and unless another boundary line is justified by special circumstances, the boundary is the median line, every point of which is
equidistant from the nearest points of the baselines from which the
breadth of the territorial sea of each State is measured.

2. Where the same continental shelf is adjacent to the territories of
two adjacent States, the boundary of the continental shelf shall be
determined by agreement between them. In the absence of agreement, and unless another boundary line is justified by special circumstances, the boundary shall be determined by application of the

principle of equidistance from the nearest points of the baseline from which the breadth of the territorial sea of each State is measured.

While Article 6 distinguishes between adjacent states and states whose coasts are opposite each other, it prescribes the same three methods of solution in either situation. Thus, the Convention suggests that the interested parties try to settle boundary disputes by agreement. However, in the absence of an agreement, unless special circumstances otherwise justify, boundaries are demarcated according to the principle of equidistance.

The provision permitting boundaries to be set by agreement appears to be superfluous, since the other rules for setting boundaries are, like most rules of international law, *jus dispositivum*, and may always be altered by agreement among interested parties. Even in the absence of the provision of Article 6 providing for an arrangement by agreement, the parties could always have recourse to this method, and delimit their portion of the continental shelf as suits them best.[1] Article 6, however, makes specific mention of that method, putting it ahead of the equidistance rule and the special circumstances exception. Thus, as observed by the International Court of Justice, agreement among the parties concerned is an obligation which must be fulfilled effectively:

The parties are under an obligation to enter in negotiations with a view to arriving at an agreement and not merely to go through a formal process of negotiation as a sort of prior condition for the automatic application of a certain method of delimitation in the absence of agreement; they are under an obligation so to conduct themselves that the negotiations are meaningful, which will not be the case when either of them insist upon its own position without contemplating any modification of it.[2]

---

[1] See *The North Sea Continental Shelf Cases, I.C.J. Reports, 1969,* p. 42: "It is well understood that, in practice, rules of international law can, by agreement, be derogated from in particular cases, or as between particular parties."

[2] *Ibid.,* p. 47. Venezuela, probably because of her special geographical situation, proposed at the Geneva Conference that limits between adjacent

The rule of equidistance or median line, which is to be applied "in the absence of agreement," is a well-known method applied in various situations: to fix state boundaries on rivers and other waterways (an alternative boundary in this situation is the middle channel line of Thalweg), and to set the limits of a state's territorial sea.[3] It is adopted by the 1964 European Fishery Convention for delimiting exclusive fishing rights. It is important to note that the median or equidistance line is often characterized as a "general rule."[4] In the opinion of the British delegate at the Geneva Conference, even in the case of special circumstances where a deviation from the median line would be justified, "the median line would provide the best starting point for negotiations."[5] It is deemed to lead mostly to equitable results, which are acceptable to the interested parties, and it is useful for avoiding protracted boundary disputes.[6] It does not, however, eliminate the need for agreement in order to set an exact boundary line.[7]

The relationship between the three methods set up in Arti-

---

states should only be set by agreement. *U.N. Conf. on the Law and the Sea, Official Records*, vol. 6 (A/CONF.13/42), at pp. 94–96, 138 (1958).

[3] Article 12 of the Geneva Convention on the Territorial Sea, where settlement by mutual agreement is only provided for as an exception.

[4] See, for instance, Sandström's statement at June 24, 1953, meeting of the International Law Commission, *Ybk. Int'l L. Comm'n 1953*, I, p. 107. See also Int'l L. Comm'n, *Report Covering the Work of its Fifth Session*, 8 U.N. GAOR, Supp. 9 (A/2456), para. 82, reprinted in *Ybk. Int'l L. Comm'n, 1953*, II, p. 216. ". . . the Commission now felt in the position to formulate a general rule, based on the principle of equidistance, applicable to the boundaries of the continental shelf both of adjacent States and of States whose coasts are opposite to each other." *Ybk. Int'l L. Comm'n., 1953*, II, p. 216.

[5] *1958 Conference on the Sea*, vol. 6 (A/CONF.13/42), p. 93.

[6] This is also recognized by the International Court of Justice, *The North Sea Continental Shelf Cases, I.C.J. Reports 1969*, p. 23.

[7] A perusal of the text of the Danish-German Agreement of June 9, 1965, which partially delimits the continental shelf between Denmark and Germany, illustrates the necessity of an explicit agreement. The coordinates of the boundary line established by the Danish-German Agreement are indicated in terms of the European Datum System, and are 55° 10′ 03,4″N and 7° 33′ 09, 6″E. If particular reference to a specified map was not indicated, serious

cle 6 of the Geneva Convention on the Continental Shelf was explained by the International Court of Justice in the recent judgment in the *North Sea Continental Shelf Cases*. The Court explained that the equidistance rule must not be considered as the principal method which should be applied after the breakdown of formal negotiations, and which should only rarely be subrogated by the exception of special circumstances. In the light of the Court's judgment, the importance of the negotiations method and that of the application of the special circumstances clause is increased; the contrary being true with regard to the equidistance rule.

## *"Special Circumstances" and Equidistance Rule*

As noted above, Article 6 provides for an exception to the principle of equidistance when special circumstances justify. However, the text of the Convention does not indicate what these special circumstances may be; what the alternative guiding principles should be; or how the existence of the special circumstances or appropriate guiding principles should be ascertained. Legislative history, in the form of discussions by the International Law Commission and at the Geneva Conference, are also unhelpful. While mention was made of islands, especially those quite distant from their owner's coast and nearer the coast of another country, mining and fishing rights,[8] and navigational sea lanes, no clear explanation of why these examples constituted

---

disputes could have occurred as the terminal point of the dividing line has Danish coordinates of 55° 10′ 01,1″N and 7° 33′ 09,6″E, and German coordinates of 55° 10′ 07,1″N and 7° 33′ 07,7″E. There could thus have been serious disputes over a longitudinal difference of 6″ and a latitudinal difference of 1.9″.

[8] Article 3 of the Convention on the Continental Shelf provides that "[t]he rights of the coastal State over the continental shelf do not affect the legal status of the superjacent waters as the high seas. . . ." Article 6, para. 7, of the same Convention, states that "neither the installations or devices, nor the safety zones around them, may be established where inter-

special circumstances was offered. The indefinite nature of the exception led to various proposals for its deletion, e.g., by the Yugoslav and British delegations.[9] As the Yugoslav delegation noted:

> . . . it is desirable to know *in advance* what criteria can be taken into consideration in drawing boundary lines, in order to avoid future misunderstandings and arbitrary interpretations. As regards the delimitation of two adjacent continental shelves, there are only two firm and solid criteria: (*a*) agreements between the States concerned and, (*b*) the principle of median lines. No other criterion is admissible and in particular no "special circumstances" can be taken into account, for their vagueness and arbitrary character could constitute a breeding ground for misunderstandings and dissensions. [Emphasis in original.] [10]

Moreover, if conflict developed, both parties would avoid activities in the contested area, thus permitting it to lie fallow. Besides, if the "exceptional circumstances" clause were too often applied —a possibility if its application is not precisely regulated—the purpose of Article 6 would be undermined. These objections, though, proved unpersuasive to the majority, and the special circumstances exception, which was primarily supported by those states expecting to gain by its application, was adopted.

It is difficult to determine what the "special circumstances" exception means. A clue may be derived from the words "special" and "justify." These words imply that the exception should not be invoked unless the area in question has such a higher degree of unusual geographical configuration that one of the adjacent states would suffer great injustice if its portion of the continental shelf were delimited according to the principle

---

ference may be caused to the use of recognized sea lanes essential to international navigation." Thus, fishing interests are sufficiently protected and need not be considered for purposes of delimitation.

[9] *1958 Conference on the Sea*, vol. 6 (A/CONF.13/42), pp. 96–98, 130, 134.
[10] *1958 Conference on the Sea*, vol. 2 (A/CONF.13/38), p. 94.

of equidistance. Features causing a coastline to be only slightly different than an idealized norm would not warrant invocation of the special circumstances rule as no coastline is identical, and all would thus be eligible for special treatment, a situation not envisioned by the framers of the Convention. After all, if a majority were excepted from a general rule, it would be hard to say that the majority received "special" treatment. Besides, minor geographical irregularties would not "justify" such deviation.

Instances in which it would be appropriate to apply the exception clause are the Channel Islands and the North Sea case. The British Channel Islands are located very near the French coast. On the basis of this situation the British part of the continental shelf would be substantially enlarged while France's would be correspondingly diminished. In that case, an application of the clause would be justified and a solution could be found by negotiations and agreement.[11]

The *North Sea Continental Shelf Cases* were quite recently pleaded before the International Court of Justice, and the Court's Judgment of February 20, 1969, gives much help in the interpretation of Article 6 of the Geneva Convention. Germany's coast is situated on that part of the North Sea where the curvature of the coast deeply recesses, while the neighboring Danish and Dutch coasts are projected relatively outward. In such a case, the effect of the use of the equidistance method is to pull the line of the boundary inward, in the direction of the concavity. The lines of equidistance meet at a relatively short distance from the coast of the disadvantaged state.[12] In the *North Sea Continental Shelf* case, the result would give Germany a

---

[11] France is also at a disadvantage in the Dover Strait and the Gulf of Biscay. Therefore, France ratified the Convention on the Continental Shelf with several reservations. See *United Nations Treaty Series*, vol. 538, p. 336.

[12] See Map 2, reproduced from the *North Sea Continental Shelf Cases, I.C.J. Reports, 1969*, p. 97.

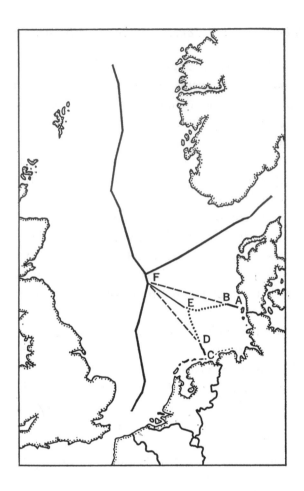

Map 2   The North Sea Continental Shelf

Lines A-B and C-D are boundaries agreed to by Germany, Denmark, and the Netherlands. Lines B-E-F and D-E-F are the boundaries that would result from the application of the equidistance principle, with the segment E-F agreed to in a treaty between Denmark and the Netherlands as reflecting their view of the correct boundary lines between their respective shelves. Lines B-F and D-F are the boundaries that Germany wished to obtain in negotiations with Denmark and the Netherlands. Thus the area bounded by F-B-E-D-F represents the difference between the claims of the parties. (Source: Map 3, *North Sea Continental Shelf Cases, I.C.J. Reports, 1969.*)

continental shelf area of 23,600 square kilometers, the Netherlands 61,800, and Denmark 61,500. Denmark and the Netherlands claimed that the delimitation of the continental shelf should be governed by the rules of Article 6 of the Convention and that the equidistance rule is applicable. However, Germany asserted that she is not bound by the Convention and that, in any case, special circumstances justified delimitation methods other than that of equidistance.

The judgment of the Court declares that the use of the equidistance method is not obligatory between the parties, and that delimitation is to be effected by agreement in accordance with equitable principles. Furthermore, the Court indicated some factors which are to be taken into account in the course of negotiations.

For our purposes here, only certain views of the Court referring to the interpretation of Article 6 and the application of the special circumstances clause will be discussed. The Court observes that in certain geographical circumstances which are quite frequently met with, the equidistance method, despite its known advantages, leads to inequity. A slight irregularity in a coastline is automatically magnified by the equidistance line. The greater the irregularity and the further from the coastline, the more unreasonable are the results produced. So great an exaggeration of the consequences of a natural geographical feature must be remedied or compensated for as far as possible, being itself creative of inequity. However,

equity does not necessarily imply equality. There can never be question of completely refashioning nature, and equity does not require that a State without access to the sea should be allotted an area of continental shelf, any more than there could be a question of rendering the situation of a State with an extensive coastline similar to that of a State with a restricted coastline.[13]

---

[13] Judgment of February 20, 1969, *I.C.J. Reports, 1969*, pp. 49–50.

In the opinion of the Court, any situation where the shares of the interested states with comparable other factors would be markedly unequal because of some irregularity of the coastline justifies a treatment "abating the effects of an incidental special feature." [14]

## *Application of Delimitation Methods for Partitioning Wider Submarine Areas*

Let us now consider the effect of applying the Continental Shelf Convention in the future, when new technical means will permit exploitation in deeper sea areas. As an extreme case, we will assume that the exploitability test has been given its most extensive interpretation, and that technological progress has reached a level at which all submarine areas are exploitable. In that case all submarine areas would be claimed by some state as continental shelf, and the question of delimitating opposing or overlapping claims would arise. Map 3 [15] demonstrates the complete division of the submarine areas of the world. Even in applying the three methods set out in Article 6 of the Convention

---

[14] The German memorial contains more maps illustrating inequalities arising from imaginary or real situations. See, e.g., Figures 11 and 12, where the location of islands brings a marked disadvantage to Albania (because of the Greek Corfu island group) and to Rumania (because of the tiny Soviet Serpent Island at a distance of about 40 km. from the coast).

[15] Map 3 is reproduced, with modifications, from "A Hypothetical Division of the Sea Floor," prepared by Robert H. Warsing for the Law of the Sea Institute, as an annex to *The Law of the Sea: Proceedings of the Second Annual Conference of the Law of the Sea Institute*, 1967. In a note to the map, F. T. Christy, Jr., and H. Herfindal state: "This map is an illustration of how the sea floor might look if it were divided along lines equidistant from the closest points of adjacent or opposite coastal states and islands. Proposals for such a division have been made as a basis for establishment of the exclusive rights that will be necessary for the encouragement and administration of the exploitation of deep sea minerals. The proposals are based on the open-ended criterion of exploitability, as expressed in the Geneva Convention on the Continental Shelf. These proposals ignore the widely held belief that an extension of rights must be limited by some concept of proximity."

Map 3    A Hypothetical Division of the Sea Floor [15]

on the Continental Shelf, as cautiously outlined in the judgment of the International Court of Justice, many anomalies will be found because some large and important countries would receive only a relatively small share, while various small countries would control areas out of all proportion to their population, coastline, and size. Neighboring countries in otherwise similar situations would receive unequal shares due to a slight irregularity of the shoreline or to the location of a promontory or an island.

*The Position of Landlocked Countries.* A hypothetical partitioning of the entire ocean floor among states possessing sea coasts would prevent the twenty-four landlocked countries,[16] possessing about 3 percent of the world's population, from sharing the riches of submarine areas. While existing law deprives these countries of the opportunity to exploit submarine resources of the internal waters, the territorial sea, and a narrowly based continental shelf, they have not suffered much greater disadvantages than those coastal countries whose small coastlines and barren seabeds yield few riches. This initial injustice becomes aggravated as the exclusive rights of individual states are expanded on a larger scale. Such a solution would be contrary to certain principles of the international law of the sea as laid down in the Geneva Convention on the High Seas and the Geneva Convention on Fishing and the Conservation of the Living Resources of the High Seas.

Article 2 of the Convention on the High Seas specifically grants four freedoms for all states, both coastal and landlocked, and implies the existence of other freedoms. Article 3 provides that, in order to enjoy the freedom of the seas on equal terms

---

[16] Twenty-nine, if some small states which are not members of the United Nations are included, i.e., Andorra, Bhutan, Liechtenstein, San Marino, Vatican City. The twenty-four landlocked countries are Afghanistan, Austria, Bolivia, Botswana, Burundi, Central African Republic, Chad, Czechoslovakia, Hungary, Laos, Lesotho, Luxemburg, Malawi, Mali, Mongolia, Nepal, Niger, Paraguay, Rwanda, Swaziland, Switzerland, Uganda, Upper Volta, and Zambia.

with coastal states, states having no seacoast should have free access to the sea. To this end, states situated between the sea and a landlocked state are to accord to the state having no seacoast free transit through their territory, and to accord ships flying the flag of the landlocked state equal treatment as regards access to and use of their ports. This principle is applied in the 1965 Geneva Convention on Transit Trade of Land-Locked Countries. Article 4 of the Convention on the High Seas proclaims that every state, whether coastal or not, has the right to sail ships under its flag on the high seas. According to the Convention on Fishing and Conservation of the Living Resources of the High Seas, nationals of every state may engage in fishing. An exaggerated extension of individual state rights over submarine areas is certainly contrary to the spirit of existing international law and of the 1958 Geneva Conventions.

It may be recalled that there is no remedy in the case of landlocked countries. As the International Court states in the *North Sea Continental Shelf Cases*, "equity does not require that a State without access to the sea should be allotted an area of continental shelf." Therefore, it would appear that landlocked countries would be unanimously against any expansion of the continental shelf beyond its natural and present legal limits.

*Isolated and Small Islands.* The Convention on the Continental Shelf provides that every island may have its own continental shelf. Therefore, states may claim sovereign rights over submarine areas surrounding all their island possessions. Although this solution is reasonable and justified if the islands are near the coast of the claiming state, it becomes questionable if the island is far from the metropolitan territory. If, like the Channel Islands, the island or group of islands is located near the coast of the claiming state but yet nearer the coast of another state, it is debatable whether the island's continental shelf should be recognized and the principle of equidistance applied. In order to decide whether the "special circumstances" clause should be applied, all such cases must be treated individually, taking into account the area, population, and economic situation of the island and of both interested countries, as well as the historical circumstances of possession and acquisition of titles.

The propriety of applying the principle of equidistance becomes even more doubtful in cases where the island or group of islands is far from the main territory of the claiming state and much nearer to the coasts of another state. For example, the Andaman and Nicobar Islands belong to India, but they are quite near the coasts of Burma, Thailand, and Indonesia; Bermuda and the Bahama Islands belong to the United Kingdom but are closer to the coast of the United States. Here, the island or group of islands is far from the coast of the claiming state and quite near the coast of another state. Of course these cases, too, may be adjusted under the special circumstances clause. The situation is even further complicated by the fact that many of these islands are now, or will soon become, independent states.[17] Results might differ depending on whether the island is independent. Thus, the French islands of St. Pierre and Miquelon would certainly be accorded shares of the continental shelf if they ever became independent,[18] just as are Western Samoa and the tiny island states of the Caribbean.

A somewhat different problem is presented by such Atlantic Ocean islands as Ascension, St. Helena, and Tristan de Cunha,[19] which are located in the middle of a large ocean far

---

[17] For example, Mauritius became independent on March 12, 1968.

[18] The location of St. Pierre and Miquelon entitles France to claim sovereign rights over part of the Grand Banks, a valuable fishing area which Canada considers exclusively within her jurisdiction. Newfoundland also claims the Grand Banks. Christy, "Realities of Ocean Resources," report presented to the Second Annual Law of the Sea Conference, Kingston, Rhode Island, 1967 (mimeographed).

[19] Similar islands are located in the Pacific and Indian Oceans. In September, 1955, a unit of the British navy landed on Rockall, in the far North Atlantic, and proclaimed the rock as a British possession. Rockall is surrounded by a fairly extensive continental shelf (in the geological sense).

from their parent state and far from any other state. While in many cases the most equitable result would be to disregard the existence of the island, each case must be considered on its own merits. At best, a general solution would only be acceptable in cases involving sparsely populated or uninhabited, small, isolated islands. Interested states would probably agree to disregard them for purposes of subdividing the continental shelf, and even if no agreement was reached such solution would probably be granted by arbitration. However, even this solution is not always clearly appropriate as it might merely shift the advantage from one country to another so that a newly favored country, instead of the original state, would get a disproportionately large shelf with regard to its area, population, and economic situation.[20]

*States Surrounding Mediterranean Seas.* The shares of the continental shelf of states bordering Mediterranean seas would be much smaller than the share of less populated states with smaller coastlines, but which are situated adjacent to open seas.[21] The situation of China is particularly striking since despite the fact that she has one of the largest superficies, the larg-

---

[20] For example, if Ascension, St. Helena, and Tristan de Cunha were disregarded, the portion of the continental shelf of Liberia, Ivory Coast, Ghana, Gabon, Angola and Southwest Africa would be enlarged, and that of Togo, Dahomey, Nigeria, and Cameroon, would remain the same.

[21] The Baltic Sea covers 382,000 square kilometers and is surrounded by seven states, and the Mediterranean Sea covers 2.5 million square kilometers and is encircled by sixteen states. In comparison, the Atlantic Ocean covers about 86 million square kilometers and is ringed by thirty-five states.

States on the Baltic Sea include Sweden, Finland, Poland, East Germany, West Germany, Denmark, and the Soviet Union. States on the Mediterranean Sea include Albania, Yugoslavia, Italy, France, Spain, Morocco, Algeria, Tunisia, Libya, Egypt, Israel, Lebanon, Syria, Turkey, Greece, Bulgaria and Romania. Corsica even further limits Italy's share, while the Greek Islands and Cyprus affect Turkey's claims. States on the Red Sea and the Persian Gulf include Egypt, Sudan, Ethiopia, Saudi Arabia, Yemen, Southern Yemen, Trucial Coast Sheikdoms, Qatar, Kuwait, Iraq and Iran. States on the Caribbean include Venezuela, Colombia, Panama, Costa Rica, Nicaragua, Honduras, Guatemala, Mexico, Jamaica, Cuba and Haiti. In the Far East states adversely affected are Thailand, Cambodia, Malaysia, Vietnam, China and Korea.

est population, and a coastline of nearly 3,500 miles, she would get a smaller share of the continental shelf than such states as Somalia, Ceylon, or Madagascar.

*States Receiving Disproportionate Shares.* Our hypothetical division would also restrict several large, populous states to disproportionately small shares of the seabed. For example, Ceylon's share would be much larger than Pakistan's and relatively larger than India's share; Indonesia, with a population greater than 100 million, would have a smaller share than Australia, Chile, or Peru; the United Kingdom would receive less than Ireland or Iceland; Canada's Atlantic coast share would be larger than the share of the United States; [22] and Cuba's share would be smaller than that of Barbados.

The inequality that we have seen results from an application of the principle of equidistance and could not be ended if another method of dividing the seabed were utilized. Even if the special circumstances exception of Article 6 were invoked, no equitable solution could be found for cases involving landlocked countries, states bordering Mediterranean seas, or coastal states receiving a disproportionately small area of the continental shelf because of their abnormal shoreline. After all, landlocked countries and states bordering on Mediterranean seas could only receive larger shares of the continental shelf if they were given rights over areas located somewhere in the oceans. This is an improbable eventuality. Similarly, it is hardly conceivable that a country bordering on a large ocean, but having a small part of the continental shelf allotted to it because of the fact that the shores of other countries are better situated, could ask for a rectification of the delimitation at the expense of its better situated neighbors.[23]

---

[22] Canada's Pacific Coast share is severely restricted by Alaska's share.

[23] For example, India's position towards Ceylon, the Maldives, and Indonesia; China's toward Korea, Japan, and the Philippines.

Other methods of subdividing the ocean floor among the coastal states have been proposed. For example, Bernfeld has suggested that "the beds of all the Great Seas shall be deemed divided by median line through the longest dimension of each, and then run each coastal nation's rights to the seabed to that median between the lines of latitude and longitude, as the case might be, from the nation's coastal extremities." [24] However, such procedure, which is rarely used in setting international boundaries, would merely shift the inequality; it would not avoid it.

The inequality in the allotment of shares of submarine areas, when the exploitability of natural resources can be extended without regard to the depth of superjacent waters, demonstrates that the literal application of the rules laid down would be unacceptable for most of the states of the world. Another method of division among states would generate similar inequalities. A partition of all existing submarine areas and the taking over of "sovereign rights" by individual coastal states is contrary to the general conception of general free access to the natural resources of these areas for all. For these reasons, even if the wording of the Convention on the Continental Shelf would permit such an interpretation, it would be highly desirable and necessary to avoid the application of the provisions now in force by agreeing on a modification of these provisions and adopting a new text which should regulate the matter in some other manner.

---

[24] Bernfeld, "Developing the Resources of the Sea," *The International Lawyer,* 1967, p. 73.

# Proposals for Revision of
the Present Law

PART III

# 7

## Proposals for a Redefinition of the Continental Shelf

THE GENERAL CONCLUSION FROM THE FOREGOING CONSIDERATIONS may be that an overall partition of the whole space of the submarine areas of the oceans is unacceptable and should be rejected. In Chapters 5 and 6 we have noted the consequences of a too liberal application of the definition of the continental shelf as laid down in Article 1 of the Geneva Convention (1958). A strictly verbal interpretation would seem to disregard other essential elements of the said definition. We do not agree with such an interpretation, but there is sufficient ground for fear that under the influence of various factors it could in fact prevail by way of state practice and precedents which would not meet a sufficiently strong opposition at the right moment.

There is, however, as explained in Chapter 6, another sounder and more logical interpretation which takes into due account the other essential elements contained in the legal definition of the continental shelf, and we have tried to arrive at a more precise formulation of the meaning of all the component elements in order to know how far the continental shelf, as defined by the Geneva Convention, could be extended in the direction of the open sea space.

We have seen that a great majority of states are or would be dissatisfied with an extensive application of Article 1 which would lead to an overall partition of the seabed and subsoil of the oceans. They would certainly support the other way, i.e., a limited extension of the exclusive rights of coastal states over the continental shelf. If we suppose that this view will prevail, and finally, as we hope, be generally accepted, two sets of questions arise:

(1) How to define that part of submarine areas which should be recognized as falling under the individual and exclusive authority of coastal states?

(2) How to determine the legal regime that should be established for the submarine areas which will not be allotted to individual coastal states?

In the present chapter we shall first consider what alternative should replace the present imprecise definition of the continental shelf as set forth in the Geneva Convention of 1958. Then, we shall consider which procedure should be used to arrive at a universal adoption of the said resolution. In this context, we shall examine whether the interested states will be disposed to accept the proposed resolution, and which procedure should be used to that effect.

## *Substitution of a Fixed Depth Limit for the Exploitability Test*

In order to give an answer to the first question, the actual text of the Geneva Convention on the Continental Shelf must be taken as the starting point. Article 1 of the Convention indicates that the continental shelf falling under the jurisdiction of the next coastal state extends as far as the 200-meter isobath, and also beyond that line if the depth of the superjacent waters admits of the exploitation of natural resources. A liberal interpretation of this provision would extend the sovereign rights of coastal states as far as the abyssal depths if and when exploitation of natural resources became feasible at such depths. Such an interpretation is rejected on the basis of the arguments which were set forth in the foregoing chapters.

The extension of exclusive rights of coastal states should be stopped at a given point, even if new technological improvements and inventions make exploitation possible beyond that point. The determination of the outer limit of exclusive national rights over submarine areas may be based on some real factors, but the choice of these factors is at least partly arbitrary. Some of these factors were reviewed before as arguments against an exaggerated extension of the continental shelf. They will now be taken up in order to determine the limit of exclusive rights of coastal states towards the rest of submarine areas whose legal regime is still to be discussed.

The first factor to be taken into account is the link between the geological concept of the continental shelf as a natural feature of the marine environment, and the legal concept as defined in Article 1 of the Geneva Convention. Although the two concepts have been separated in the codification work of the Geneva Conference it is nevertheless true that the claims to exercise sovereign rights over enlarged portions of submarine areas have been supported and justified by the thesis that the portions concerned represent a natural extension of the adjacent land, that the seabed of offshore areas is but a submerged part of the land belonging to the country which is situated on the shores thereof.[1] The same argument cannot be advanced in favor of claims to exclusive rights over more distant areas.

---

[1] The judgment in the *North Sea Continental Shelf Cases, I.C.J. Reports, 1969*, repeatedly refers to the relevance of the natural prolongation or continuation of the land domain. See paras. 43, 44, and 85; "The continental shelf of any State must be the natural prolongation of its land territory"; para. 95: "The institution of the continental shelf has arisen out of the recognition of a physical fact; and the link between this fact and the law, without which that institution would never have existed, remains an important element for the application of its legal régime".

On the basis of the above considerations we may say that the exclusive rights of coastal states must find their limit at the point where it can no longer be asserted that the submarine areas are a natural continuation of the land mass.

In theory, the most reasonable solution would be to determine the legal limit of the continental shelf by the natural feature of the marine environment near the coast. Yet, in practice, this would not give a reliable basis. As explained in Chapter 2 there is no unanimity in determining the extent of the continental shelf. There may be two or three steps in the fall-off of the seabed; trenches and canyons may interrupt the uniformity of the profiles; and differences may arise about the question whether the slope should be annexed to the shelf as its part or whether the shelf should end on the line where the gradient becomes steeper. Finally, and probably the most important, the fall-off of the shelf does not occur everywhere at the same depth. Consequently, some states would get areas to a depth limit of 200 meters and more, while others would be barred at a depth line of 65 meters.

For all these reasons the choice of the natural phenomenon as a basis for the determination of the outer limit of exclusive national rights is impracticable. Therefore, states have determined the limit of their claims by a fixed depth. Such a limit can easily be verified: if a given spot of the seabed lies under waters deeper than the indicated limit, it does not belong to the domain of individual exclusive rights of the nearest coastal state.

The choice of a uniform isobath as the limit of individual exclusive rights has the advantage that it gives equal chances to all, so long as the exploitability does not reach depths beyond the isobath. If a state happens to have near its coast a narrow band of shallow seas, it loses nothing in comparison to another state whose continental shelf extends tens or hundreds of miles towards the open sea. The first would gain nothing by having its own submarine areas extended to the isobath of 400 or more meters, because it could not exploit the resources of that area.

## The Choice of the Isobath

Having decided that a uniform isobath should be the best limit, the next question concerns the choice of the isobath. In the Convention on the Continental Shelf the isobath of 200 meters has been chosen. At that time, oil drilling could not be undertaken in depths exceeding 100 meters. Yet, it should be remembered that oil drilling is not the only kind of exploitation. Moreover, drilling methods have been improved, and it is possible that very soon drillings far beyond the isobath of 200 meters could yield commercially interesting quantities of oil. On the other hand, if the exploitability reaches greater depths, a coastal state could exploit areas beyond the isobath. But if that is the limit of its exclusive rights and the seabed's fall-off happens to occur near the coast, it is at a disadvantage by comparison with those states whose submarine areas inside the isobath are more extensive.

In such a situation the remedy would be to increase the yardstick of the isobath, i.e., to choose a new isobath covering all exploitable areas. But this remedy would be provisional only, because new technological progress may advance anew the limits of exploitability. Therefore, this solution would not be satisfactory, and we shall consider a remedy for the inequality which would be the effect of a simple application of the isobath limit. There were proposals before the Geneva Conference of 1958, and at the conference itself, to increase the isobath limit 300 to 500 meters and more. Actually, the Dutch branch of the International Law Association has proposed the 500-meter isobath as boundary "for practical reasons." [2] The same limit is also pro-

---

[2] International Law Association, *Report of the Fifty-Second Conference, 1966*, p. 797. The American Branch of the International Law Association argues for an extension of the continental shelf to a depth of 2,500 meters or a distance of 100 miles, whichever limitation encompasses the larger area. Committee on Deep Sea Mineral Resources, *Interim Report*, July 19, 1968, p. XVIII. See a dissenting opinion by L. Henkin, *ibid.*, p. XXI.

posed by the association's committee on deep-sea mining. Senator Pell's proposal in S. Res. 186 runs as follows:

In order to assure freedom of the exploration and exploitation of ocean space and its resources as provided in these principles, there is a clear necessity that fixed limits must be set for defining the outer boundaries of the continental shelf of coastal States. For the purpose of these principles, the term "continental shelf" is used as referring (a) to the seabed and subsoil of the submarine areas adjacent to the coast but outside the area of the territorial sea to a depth of 600 meters, and (b) to the seabed and subsoil of similar areas adjacent to the coasts of islands.[3]

Senator Pell, in a subsequent version [4] submitted to the Senate in the form of a Declaration to be sponsored by the United States delegation in the United Nations Seabed Committee, proposed an important alteration, namely, the extension of the continental shelf "to the seabed and subsoil of the submarine areas adjacent to the coast but outside the area of the territorial sea to a depth of 550 metres, *or to a distance of 50 miles* from the baseline from which the breadth of the territorial sea is measured, whichever results in the greatest area of the continental shelf." (Emphasis added).

Many people would object that an extension of the isobath from 200 to 500 or 600 meters is contrary to the main objective of the proposed amendment to the Geneva Convention, and that it encroaches upon the domain which should be reserved as common to all mankind. But, although we agree that an exaggerated extension of individual national shores in the continental shelf should be avoided, the above mentioned extension would not cover an important part of the oceans. The geographical data

---

[3] S. Res. 186, 90th Cong., 1st Sess., *Congressional Record*, vol. 113, p. 33020. This was later embodied in Senator Pell's Ocean Space Draft Treaty (Art. 29). See S. Res. 263, 90th Cong., 2nd Sess., *ibid.*, vol. 114, p. 5181.

[4] S. Res. 33, 91st Cong., 1st Sess., *Congressional Record*, vol. 115, p. 1330 (January 21, 1969).

about the repartition of depths in the sea show that the bracket of depths between 200 meters and 1,000 meters amounts to only 4.3 percent of the total area of the seas. Taking that into account, we may conclude that even a limit of 500 meters or a little more would not take an excessive part from the free sea areas. In the present author's opinion, to admit the extension of sovereign rights to greater depths would be justified only as a means to get a sure majority of votes for amending the actual text of the Geneva Convention. But if it could be avoided, it would be better to abide by the actual 200-meter isobath.[5] The following reasons reinforce this solution:

*Combination of Depth with Distance Criterion.* It has been explained that the continental shelf is unequally distributed around the world. The same is true with respect to the depths of the sea near the coast. At some points the sea extends far away from the coast before attaining the depth of 200 meters, at other points the fall to greater depths is more abrupt, and deep seas are quite near to the coast. As a consequence, some states get a large area as their continental shelf, and some states have no continental shelf at all because the depth of the waters, even inside their territorial waters, exceed 200 meters. This fact was one of the reasons for inserting the exploitability test into the definition of Article 1 of the Convention on the Continental Shelf.

In order to remedy the disadvantage of states with no, or small, continental shelves, some states have sought to extend their jurisdiction to areas delimited by a given distance from the coast. The most excessive claims were those of some Latin American states extending their authority (defined sometimes as sovereignty) as far as 200 miles from the coast. The determination of

---

[5] Another argument against raising the isobath limit beyond 200 meters is that the possibility of profitable exploitation decreases as water depth increases. Thus, the size of the fund collected by an international agency, and to be used for aiding developing countries, would be diminished.

the exclusive rights of coastal states by a fixed distance from the coast would give satisfaction to these states which have no continental shelf at all or whose continental shelf does not extend far from the outer limit of their territorial sea.

It is true that the allotment of areas with greater depths will have no practical effect so long as natural resources of the seabed and subsoil cannot be exploited at greater depths. However, today it is almost certain that the exploitation in greater depths will become feasible in the fairly near future. The additional recognition of sovereign rights to a determined distance from the coast would therefore represent a sort of compensation for states whose continental shelf (or the areas with depths less than 200 meters) is small or nonexistent. A distance of 30 miles would be the best measure. This was proposed by some authors at the very beginning of the discussion on the problem of the continental shelf.[6]

As a result of these considerations, it is submitted that a new definition of the continental shelf in its legal sense, i.e., as the submarine areas where individual states exercise sovereign rights with respect to the exploration and exploitation of natural resources, should be based on two precise criteria: an isobath, and a distance from the coast. Every state would be entitled *ipso jure* to the exercise of sovereign rights (for the purpose of exploring and exploiting natural resources of the seabed and its subsoil) up to a depth of 200 meters, but also beyond this limit to a distance of 30 miles from the coast. This may also be formulated inversely: to a distance of 30 miles from the coast, and beyond this limit to a depth of 200 meters. These figures may be altered if this should be necessary to reach international agreement.

---

[6] Azcarraga, "Los derechos sobre la plataforma submarina," *Revista Española de Derecho Internacional,* 1949, p. 47; Mateesco, *Le droit international nouveau,* 1948; and the Report of the French Branch of the International Law Association at the Copenhagen Conference, 1950. It may be recalled that some authors consider 30 miles as the average width of the continental shelf. See Chapter 1, p. 9.

Such a solution was advocated by the present writer in 1951.[7] Today it finds many adherents. The author here favors a delimitation of the continental shelf which is as narrow as possible. One of the reasons is the fact that the distribution of submarine areas among coastal states always results in unavoidable inequalities. Every increase in the size of the individual parts increases these inequalities as well.[8] For these and other reasons, the individual continental shelf parts of coastal states should not be extended beyond a reasonable measure.

The adjacency criterion is well suited to limit extended claims. In a recent study Louis Henkin argues for a delimitation of the continental shelf as narrow as possible, preferably a 200-meter isobath with a minimum shelf for all nations of X miles from the coast.[9] These two elements of delimitation could be combined so that the continental shelf would end at the 200-meter isobath. But in the deep sea beyond that limit coastal states would have a "buffer zone" up to X miles from shore from which foreign mining would be excluded. The seabed would belong to everyone or no one, depending on what the new regime provides. Automatic sovereign rights for the coastal state could be expressly rejected. If the new regime requires a royalty or tax be paid, payment would be due from this zone as well. If a license is required, or if other measures must be taken to support mining in the deep sea, it would be required in this zone as well. But whatever the regime, the coastal state alone would have the right to exploit the resources of this area.[10]

The formula of 200 isobath plus X miles from the coast is also used by the Maltese proposal in the Seabed Committee.

[7] J. Andrassy, *Epikontinentalni pojas*, 1951, pp. 67 and 68.

[8] "The wider the area of coastal claims, the more coastal nations win at the expense of inland nations. In other words, the greater the inequality through accidents of geography." Neild, "Alternative Forms of International Regime for the Oceans," *Towards a Better Use of the Oceans* (ed. by the International Institute for Peace and Conflict Research, Stockholm), 1968, p. 284.

[9] Henkin, *Law for the Sea's Mineral Resources*, 1968, pp. 72–73.

[10] *Ibid.*, pp. 46–47.

Moreover, the Maltese proposal specifies that rocks and islands without a permanent population shall not be taken into account.[11]

The United Nations Committee of the World Peace Through Law Center has suggested in a draft treaty that the limit of the continental shelf be set at the 200-meter isobath, or at 50 miles from the coast, whichever is greater.

As we have seen, the combination of depth and distance criteria may be given cumulatively or alternatively. In the latter case, some proposals prescribe the alternative that gives to the coastal state the larger area. It could be argued that a choice should be given to the coastal state concerned, since it could be in its interest to choose a smaller area (for instance, the area limited by the depth line) where exploitation seems to be more promising.

*Procedural Alternatives for a Revision of the Present Law.* Now we shall examine briefly whether the governments would be disposed to agree upon a solution as previously outlined. In doing this we envisage a possible discussion in a conference or in the General Assembly, although in Chapter 8 other possible solutions are also discussed.

The proposal that the criterion of exploitability be deleted from the definition in Article 1 would probably be supported by a large majority. An indication in this sense may be found in the discussion which took place in the First Committee of the General Assembly during its twenty-second session, when the Committee discussed the Maltese proposal on peaceful utilization of the natural resources of the sea outside the continental shelf for the benefit of mankind. The proposal met with the almost general approval of the delegates, and it is hardly conceivable that there would be serious opposition against the first amending clause—which would remove the exploitability test from the de-

---

[11] See below, pp. 127–28.

finition of the continental shelf. The great number of states which are completely barred from access to larger portions of the oceans, together with the states whose situation on the ocean shores does not secure for them a fair share, would form a solid and overwhelming majority group for this proposal.

The isobath as the unique criterion for delimiting the outward extension of the continental shelf would also be accepted by a majority. Serious opposition would come from states without an extended continental shelf. Therefore, the adoption of the isobath limit would be easier if a supplementary limit were fixed by the measured distance from the coast. A proposal combining the depth and the distance criteria would be satisfactory and acceptable to a great majority.

Greater difficulties would arise about the choice of the isobath. Probably the participating governments would determine their attitude with a view to their own situation and interests. It is not only the geographical situation which matters. The level of its industrial and financial development would be a factor in the decision of a state on the question which isobath and which distance from the coast should be chosen for the delimitation of the continental shelf.

Very often opinions are heard that the one or the other proposed solution is contrary to the interests of one group of states and advantageous to another. With respect to the question of the continental shelf and of the exploitation of natural resources in this area, as well as in the remaining areas of the seas and oceans, special stress is laid on the interests of the developing countries. There are, however, divergent views on the question whether the developing countries would be better off if they disposed of a large sector of submarine areas as their proper domain of jurisdiction. During the debates of the First Committee of the General Assembly in 1967, different views on this question were expressed by delegates of developing countries. The general impression, however, appears to be that developing countries are in favor of an international regime for submarine areas outside the continental shelf and of a limited definition of the shelf. This position appears more clearly from the attitudes expressed during the 1968 and 1969 sessions of the General Assembly, and especially from an analysis of the recorded votes on Resolution 2574 D.[12] Only one developing country (Ghana) voted against.

*How to Obtain the Greatest Possible Consensus of States.* How the proposed solution—or any similar solution—can be attained is an extremely delicate question which should be handled with care and caution. The essence of the solution proposed here is to eliminate the criterion of exploitability which, because of the elasticity in its application, is the main stumbling block. In applying that criterion the extension of the coastal states' exclusive rights could gradually advance to undesirable limits. Two principal ways are open to avoid it. One way would be to delete the exploitability criterion in the definition of Article 1 by a formal amendment of the Geneva Convention and to introduce in the definition such elements as would be agreed upon. To that effect a special conference should be convened. Another way would be to give to the exploitability criterion a restrictive interpretation on the basis of the sense of the definition as a whole, and taking into account all of its elements.

In handling the question of a better definition of the continental shelf, by interpretation or amendment, it is important that the solution be obtained with the consensus of all states concerned, or at least without open opposition. In the present author's opinion this might be possible. The United Nations is the appropriate forum for unofficial and official negotiations seeking a satisfactory solution for all.[13]

---

[12] The operative part of G. A. Res. 2574 D is set forth, *infra*, at p. 127.

[13] See Schachter, "Scientific Advance and International Law Making," *California Law Review*, May, 1967, p. 423, at 425–26: "The procedures of treaty negotiations can generate and stimulate claims for exclusive national competence which might not otherwise be made. Government representatives, faced

The double objective—widely supported from many sides and spelled out before the General Assembly by Malta—of declaring the natural resources of deep submarine areas as common heritage of mankind, and of using the benefits therefrom for the aid of developing countries, is very persuasive. Even states which could have some motive for opposing views would give way under the influence of a strong public opinion in favor of a better solution. A large individual share in the continental shelf may be a strong asset, but in many cases it has been proven that it is preferable to rely upon international cooperation than upon exclusive national assets.

Action for finding a better definition of the continental shelf should be initiated immediately (in fact it has begun already). The longer the delay, the greater the danger that the situation would develop beyond control. Belated remedies would be worse than solutions obtained at the right moment.

Alternatively, a solution might be reached in different ways. There could be informal agreements or the adoption of identical standards by the various states with respect to the definition of the continental shelf, or there could be informal negotiations through different channels. It is also possible that a competent group of personalities might examine the question of which interpretation should be given to the said definition, and that their conclusions would serve as guide for the states' practices. The group might be a scientific association such as the Institut de droit International, or the International Law Association, or a group of personalities interested in international politics or in the

---

with the prospect of formal binding commitments which are to have long duration and which require legislative approval, feel impelled to press vigorously for national rights and to avoid concessions which appear to encroach on sovereignty. This happened in the Conference on the Law of the Sea, even to the derogation of established customary law.

"In contrast to this, States may be more willing to adopt declaratory resolutions in the framework of international organizations precisely because they have the character of general statements and therefore do not purport to circumscribe the activities of states as much as detailed treaty provisions."

maintenance of peace. Among such groups are the Interparliamentary Union or the Pugwash Conference. A more authoritative form of interpretation would be a resolution adopted by the United Nations General Assembly, possibly based on the opinion of the International Law Commission, or of an *ad hoc* panel of experts, or of the International Court of Justice.

The main argument for such an interpretation could be the fact that the criterion of exploitability must be understood in connection with other elements contained in the definition of Article 1. Thus, the exploitability test should not be valid for extensions which go far beyond the geological features of the continental shelf concept or far beyond the 200-meter isobath, which would abandon the criterion of adjacency. If agreement in principle were reached in this respect, it would be possible to agree on a determined maximum distance from the coast beyond which the exploitability test would no longer be applicable.

Another way of reaching the desired solution would be an amendment of the Convention on the Continental Shelf as it is outlined in the Convention itself. All four Geneva Conventions to the Law of the Sea provide that a procedure for their revision may be initiated after the expiration of a period of five years. Article 13 of the Convention on the Continental Shelf provides as follows:

1. After the expiration of a period of five years from the date on which this Convention shall enter into force, a request for the revision of this question may be made at any time by any contracting party by means of a notification in writing addressed to the Secretary-General of the United Nations.
2. The General Assembly of the United Nations shall decide upon the steps, if any, to be taken in respect of such request.

The date limit in Article 13 refers only to the right of any single state to initiate a revision. This right cannot be exercised before the expiration of the five year period. However, the Convention does not prevent group action by the contracting parties, especially when acting as the General Assembly of the United Nations. The formality provided for in Article 13 is not necessary if the General Assembly is already considering the problem. Thus it may decide "upon the steps" even before the expiration of the said period.[14]

As already mentioned, speed would appear to be necessary. A first and preliminary step could be to freeze the extension of national claims to submarine areas as continental shelves until a definitive agreement on the question of the outer limits of the continental shelf can be reached. Such a freezing could be brought about either by a resolution of the United Nations General Assembly, or by a declaration signed by the states which are parties to the Convention on the Continental Shelf.

As a substitute to such a declaration, agreed upon by all concerned, there could, failing such a general agreement, be envisaged declarations by single states or groups of states making perfectly clear and universally known that the majority of states —an overwhelming majority if our guess is right—will never recognize excessive claims as they could result from a liberal interpretation of the definition in Article 1. States should by every possible means make known that they accept only a definition of the continental shelf which takes into reasonable account the element of adjacency contained in the said definition. In this way the definitive settlement of the question, i.e., a generally acceptable definition of the continental shelf, would be easier. The states having a favorable geographic situation could not affirm that a new definition deprives them of a claim extending to the mid-ocean, and they could not therefore ask for compensation for this pretended loss.

---

[14] The present author agrees with Henkin, *supra* note 8, at p. 39, n. 120: "By its terms any participant may seek revision five years after the Convention comes into effect. . . . Of course, there is nothing to prevent all the parties from agreeing to revise it at any time." The above considerations, written in 1968, have by now only an academic interest.

This step could be taken without delay, individually and collectively. Collective declarations could be made by regional groups, or by groups having the same interest, such as landlocked or Mediterranean states. The best form of a collective statement would be a resolution voted by the General Assembly of the United Nations. Another way to obtain an authoritative statement would be a request for an advisory opinion of the International Court of Justice. During the Twenty-third Session of the General Assembly several proposals were made to this effect.

A draft resolution proposed by Malta, Mauritius, and Tanzania would appeal to "all States to refrain from any action which may impair the extent of the area beyond limits of national jurisdiction, before the area and its juridical status are more precisely defined." [15] Another proposal, made by Cyprus and Uruguay, aimed at the adoption of a resolution in which the General Assembly:

1. Urges all States to give high priority to the question of clarifying the definition of the "continental shelf" in Article 1 of the Convention on the Continental Shelf, in accordance with the relevant appropriate procedures.

2. Requests all States to refrain from claiming or exercising sovereign rights over any part of the seabed and ocean floor, and the subsoil thereof, beyond the limits of national jurisdiction, pending the said clarification of the Convention on the Continental Shelf and without prejudice to any existing claims concerning the limits of the territorial sea or the continental shelf.

3. Declares that no acts or activities of a State, or under its authority, in the seabed or the ocean floor, or the subsoil thereof, beyond the limits of national jurisdiction which take place pending the clarification of the Convention on the Continental Shelf shall be deemed to constitute a basis of asserting any claims to those areas.[16]

---

[15] Document A/C.1/L.433 (November 5, 1968).
[16] Document A/C.1/L.432/Rev.1 (November 5, 1968).

As a consequence of various such proposals, the General Assembly, at the Twenty-fourth Session, adopted Resolution 2574 D (December 15, 1969), wherein it declared that, pending the establishment of an international régime for the exploitation of the seabed and the subsoil beyond the limits of national jurisdiction,

(a) States and persons, physical or juridical, are bound to refrain from all activities of exploitation of the resources of the area of the sea-bed and ocean floor, and the subsoil thereof, beyond the limits of national jurisdiction;

(b) No claim to any part of that area or its resources shall be recognized.

This resolution was adopted by 62 votes in favor, 28 against, with 28 abstentions. It is to be noted that the votes cast against were almost all by developed countries, including all major powers. Nevertheless, the least legal effect that can be attributed to that resolution is that the countries which voted for it have in this way declared that they are not willing to recognize new, extended claims to areas envisaged by the resolution. To that extent, the resolution serves as a valid substitute for the individual or collective protests which could be lodged against extended claims. Contrary to the situation that was witnessed at the time when the first claims to the continental shelf arose, when no protests were lodged against claims (with the exception of some exaggerated ones), in the present situation, states advancing new claims will not be able to avail themselves of the absence of protests.

Another recent proposal for an even stronger step was made by Malta in the Seabed Committee established by Resolution 2467 (XXIII). It proposed that the General Assembly should declare which part of the seabed underlying the high seas and of its subsoil "unquestionably are and must remain beyond national

jurisdiction." The limit between the parts under national jurisdiction and these parts should be determined by the 200-meter
isobath and by a distance from the nearest coast which the draft
proposal left open to discussion. Moreover, Malta proposed that
the Secretary-General should be asked to hold consultations
with member states, with the International Law Commission,
and with intergovernmental organizations, including the Intergovernmental Oceanographic Commission, on the feasibility of
convening an international conference to revise the 1958 Geneva
Convention on the Continental Shelf, and formulate legal norms
for the conduct of states in the exploration and use of the
seabed.[17] In its Resolution 2574 A (XXIV), the General Assembly took a step in this direction by requesting the Security
Council to enter into consultations with member states on the
desirability of convening a conference to review the legal
régimes of the seas and continental shelf.[18]

---

[17] Document A/AC.138/11 (March 18, 1969).
[18] See, for the text of G. A. Res. 2574 A, *infra*, p. 143–44.

# 8

## Proposals for the Control of the Deep Ocean Space: The Case for International Control

~~~~~~~~~~~~~~~~~~~~~~~~~~~~~~~~~~~~~~~~~~~~~~~~~~~~~~~~~~~

An INTERNATIONAL AGREEMENT ON A NEW DEFINITION OF THE continental shelf may stop the gradual extension of individual national rights over ever larger parts of the submarine areas. It cannot, however, stop the technological progress and prevent the growing possibilities of exploration and exploitation of the natural resources of the seabed and its subsoil in regions with ever deeper superjacent waters. As soon as some kind of exploitation of these resources becomes technically feasible and commercially rewarding, enterprise will seize this occasion and proceed to exploit the respective resources by drilling, dredging, or some other method already known or yet to be invented for that purpose. Consequently, human activities will take place in submarine areas outside the national parts of the continental shelf.

Since these areas will not be under the authority of any state, the question is how an order can be established which will avoid possible clashes between different exploring and exploiting groups. The simple application of the rules governing surface navigation and fisheries and culminating in the principle of the freedom of the high seas may soon turn out to be inadequate and insufficient. This is true even if we contemplate only activities concerning the exploration and exploitation of the natural resources of the seabed and its subsoil in a narrower sense. It is, however, probable that besides the exploration and exploitation of natural resources other human activities will develop in deep seas and on the seabed. We have especially in mind sea farming (aquiculture), communications and transport, utilization of the dynamic forces of the sea for energy production, and various national and international administrative and other services such as charting or weather forecasting.

A separate concern is the use of the deep sea, the seabed, and probably the subsoil, too, for military purposes, warning and other defence installations. Summing up, one may say that the deep sea and the seabed could in a couple of decades be the theater of many human activities whose operations could not exist without an elaborate system of regulations. As there is no state authority to do it, this system ought to be provided by international law. This could develop in part through the formation of customary rules, but for the greater part it would have to take the form of international agreements or legislative activity of an international authority.

It might be objected that the activities in submarine areas do not need a special international regime. The existing rules governing the high sea could be applied to these activities too. This solution, however, would on the one hand hamper the exploitation of natural resources and on the other hand lead to anarchic and chaotic conditions. Suppose that a company has undertaken large-scale explorations of the seabed and its subsoil, and finally it discovers a spot where the exploitation is technically feasible and commercially rewarding. It is not necessary to ask for a license, because the principle of the freedom of the high seas allows every reasonable use of the sea. The company establishes its installations on the surface or on the bottom of the sea. Both the exploration stage and the installations require large capital investments. But now, as the establishment of installations indicates that the area is promising, other companies may come and construct their installations nearby and in this way make undue profit by using the results of the costly explorations undertaken by the first company. The same might happen in cases of successful industrial espionage. The principle of the freedom of the high seas admits such interference. Under such conditions nobody would engage in explorations, and the natural resources would remain untapped.

Even greater would be the inconveniences of an absence of special regulation if we have in mind the possible implications of an intensive use of the seabed and the deeper parts of the sea, not only for exploration and exploitation but for communications and other purposes. The order of the oceans is, in the present conditions of surface navigation and fishing, assured by the rule that every state has jurisdiction over, and responsibility for, the vessels flying its flag. Control on the surface is relatively easy and has hitherto functioned satisfactorily. But in the depth of the sea identification will be more difficult, even in conditions of good will and friendship. In the case of evil intentions and wrong-doing the offender may easily escape identification and responsibility.

## Critique of the "Flag State" Approach

A solution that is sometimes suggested would give the jurisdiction and responsibility to the state whose nationals are engaged in research and exploitation on a certain place in the submarine areas. According to this "flag state" approach, the state whose vessels or other crafts or installations undertake exploratory and exploiting activities acquires some sort of authority (jurisdiction, control, or sovereignty) over the place where the said activities take place. It would be a kind of territorial authority lasting as long as the vessels and other means of exploration and exploitation flying the flag of the state concerned are actively involved in such activities in the area concerned.

This solution would confer great advantages on the developed nations, which could be used in an abusive manner. Fictitious activities could be displayed in order to acquire a priority right on potentially economically rewarding places. Recourse to flags of convenience could lead to situations as they have been experienced in navigation. Moreover, this solution would require some international regulation which would, perhaps, be more difficult to set up than a more acceptable solution. In order to avoid conflicts on the spot, there should exist a register for established claims and a set of regulations.

Our conclusion is that a clear-cut legal order for the regions of the ocean space and for the exploitation of its natural resources must be established. Thus the question arises what sort of regime would be most appropriate. This is the subject of many discussions by scholars, publicists, and diplomats. In this study we shall try to expose only some important points of possible solutions and to give some suggestions by indicating existing or proposed forms of international organization.

## Survey of Proposals for an International Regime for Submarine Areas

The question of an international regime for submarine areas which became accessible to human activities appeared as early as the problem of the continental shelf itself.[1]

In the period during which the rules concerning the continental shelf were elaborated, various proposals were made in

---

[1] In fact, as early as 1934, the Institut de Droit International, on the basis of a report by Strupp and Gidel, adopted a resolution recommending the creation, by multilateral agreement, of a permanent international organization which would establish a legal regime for the sea responsive to the common interest of the international community. An Office of the Sea would also assist states in settling conflicts and would study the legal problems of the sea. *Annuaire de l'Institut de droit international*, vol. 38, 1934, pp. 711–13. For the reports, see *Annuaire*, vol. 35, I, 1929, pp. 155–228; vol. 36, I, 1931, pp. 6–24; vol. 37, 1932, pp. 65–66. For the debate, see *Annuaire*, vol. 38, 1934, pp. 545–71.

favor of an international regime. The proposals went in three principal directions. The most radical wished to entrust an international organization with the exploitation of the natural resources of the continental shelf. Two arguments were advanced in support of this idea. First, the resources of the seabed and subsoil of the high seas were *res communis*, the property of the whole of mankind should be exploited for the benefit of mankind as a whole.

Second, from the point of view of the organization, the proponents were able to indicate a new and encouraging example in the recently created European Coal and Steel Community. Among the promoters of this kind of solution we may quote Professor Albert de Lapradelle in an opinion given before the French branch of the International Law Association and advocated with fervor at the Association's Conference in Copenhagen 1950. He proposed to entrust the organization of exploration, development and distribution of all resources of submarine areas to the United Nations. At the Copenhagen Conference he was joined by other speakers.[2] One member of the International Law Commission, Shuhsi Hsu, was also in favor of such a solution.[3]

A third trend of proposals was in favor of an international administrative authority which would grant licenses for exploration and exploitation of submarine natural resources all over the world.

A fourth category of proposals limits the task of an international agency to a supervisory and consultative activity. This idea appears, for instance, in the comments of the Dutch govern-

---

[2] International Law Association, *Report on the Forty-Fourth Conference, Copenhagen, 1950,* pp. 91–103.

[3] Meeting on July 12, 1950, *Ybk. Int'l L. Comm'n, 1950,* I, pp. 215–16. In Hsu's opinion "high seas were the property of the international community. Why then not entrust the development of the continental shelf resources to the international community? Why not a joint exploitation of these resources?"

ment on the draft articles of the International Law Commission. They recognize that "in theory it might perhaps be preferable to give jurisdiction over these submarine areas to the international community as a whole," but feel "that the practical difficulties of doing so would prove insuperable." The reason for this is also given:

Such a system would indeed make it impossible to exploit submarine resources properly in the interests of mankind. . . . [But the Dutch Government continues that it] would like to suggest that an international body should be established to control and advise on the progressive exploitation of the submarine areas, so as to promote the most effective use of these resources in the general interest.[4]

The fourth type of proposals found some approval on the part of the International Law Commission. The Commission explained its views on the problem of internationalization in its *Report Covering the Work of the Eighth Session:*

Although for the reasons stated, as well as for practical considerations, the Commission was unable to endorse the idea of internationalization of the submarine areas comprised in the concept of the continental shelf, it did not discard the possibility of setting up an international body for scientific research and assistance with a view to promoting their most efficient use in the general interest. It is possible that some such body may one day be set up within the framework of an existing international organization.[5]

As another reason, the Commission stated that the proposed internationalization "would not ensure the effective exploitation of natural resources necessary to meet the needs of mankind." [6]

---

[4] François, *Regime of the High Seas: Fourth Report (The Continental Shelf and Related Subjects)*, A/CN.4/60, at 43, reprinted in *Ybk. Int'l L. Comm'n, 1953*, II, p. 16.

[5] *Int'l L. Comm'n, Report Covering the Work of its Eighth Session*, 11 U.N. *GAOR*, Supp. 9 (A/3159), at 43, *Ybk. Int'l L. Comm'n, 1956*, II, at 298.

[6] *Ibid.* at 40, *Ybk. Int'l L. Comm'n, 1956*, II, at 296.

The creation of an international agency was proposed at the Conference on Petroleum and the Sea at Monte Carlo in 1965. In a paper on the regime on the continental shelf, Guarino and Kojanec declared themselves in favor of establishing, by international agreement, an agency acting in the interest of the international community with respect to resources which belong to that community. The oil industries, which are mostly multinational, would operate on the basis of international licenses. The said agency could issue unifom regulations for the exploitation of resources and fix the royalties which could constitute a solid financial basis for the activities of several existing international organizations.[7]

At the Geneva Conference itself voices were raised in favor of some form of internationalization. This idea was supported by Paul de Lapradelle, the delegate of Monaco. He supported the creation of an international organization as a consultative and advisory body which would help governments in the adoption of decisions fully consistent with the law of the sea.[8] His suggestions were not pursued. Germany made a formal proposal to set up a body of rules regulating the exploitation of the natural resources of submarine areas of the high seas. The observation of these rules should be secured by the coastal state closest to the installation erected for the purposes of exploration or exploitation. That state should act on behalf of the international community. Regional agreements could be entered into by the interested states in order to delimit the areas of supervision and to provide for the establishment of joint bodies empowered to perform the supervisory functions in place of the coastal state.[9] The proposal was opposed by several delegations and abandoned.

---

[7] Guarino and Kojanec, "Régime juridique du plateau continental," *Revue pétrolière*, Vol. 2, p. 201.

[8] *United Nations Conference on the Law of the Sea, Official Records,* 1958, vol. 6 (A/CONF.13/42), at p. 18.

[9] *Ibid.,* at p. 125–26.

If we accept the idea of an international regime in principle, the question remains which kind of regime should be established for the areas that will remain outside the national jurisdiction of coastal states. In this respect very important suggestions have been made quite recently and the problem is under study and discussion at the highest level, that is, in the United Nations.

## United Nations Initiatives

The initial impetus for the United Nations study was provided by Economic and Social Council Resolution 1112 (XL), of March 7, 1966. Among many topics concerning natural resources and their development, the Council conceived of a five-year survey program as a contribution to the United Nations Development Decade. One of the points in that program was a survey of offshore mineral potential in developing countries. The Secretary-General was requested to make a survey of the present state of knowledge of the resources beyond the continental shelf, excluding fish, and the techniques used in their exploitation. The Secretary-General submitted, pursuant to this resolution, a voluminous report in February, 1968.[10] This resolution was endorsed by General Assembly Resolution 2172 (XXI) of December 6, 1966, on resources of the sea, which also requested the Secretary-General to undertake a survey of the activities in marine science and technology undertaken by member states, intergovernmental organizations, and scientific and technological organizations. Moreover, the Secretary-General was directed to formulate proposals, in the light of this comprehensive study, for:

(a) Ensuring the most effective arrangements for an expanded programme of international co-operation to assist in a better under-

---

[10] *Resources of the Sea* (Beyond the Continental Shelf), E/4449, with two add; Add. 1 on mineral resources, Add. 2 on food resources.

standing of the marine environment through science and the exploitation and development of marine resources, with due regard to the conservation of fish stocks;

(b) Initiating and strengthening marine education and training programmes, bearing in mind the close interrelationship between marine and other sciences.

To this end, the General Assembly requested the Secretary-General to set up a small group of experts to assist him in the preparation of the survey and proposals. The report of the Secretary-General was published at the end of April, 1968.[11]

During 1967, United Nations involvement was widened by a Soviet proposal submitted in April to the Intergovernmental Oceanographic Commission of UNESCO. It requested the creation of a special working group to prepare a convention on international norms for exploration and exploitation of the mineral resources of the high seas. In October, 1967, the Commission adopted a resolution establishing a working group on legal questions related to scientific investigations in the ocean.

## The Maltese Proposal

At the same time the central problem of the exploitation of the natural resources of submarine areas was brought to the attention of the United Nations General Assembly. In an explanatory memorandum dated August 17, 1967,[12] the Maltese government suggested that the General Assembly put on its agenda a topic entitled "The Declaration and Treaty Concerning the Reservation Exclusively for Peaceful Purposes of the Seabed and the Ocean Floor, Underlying the Seas Beyond the Limits of Present National Jurisdiction, and the Use of Their Resources in the Interests of Mankind." The Maltese government explained:

---

[11] *Marine Science and Technology: Survey and Proposals,* E/4487.
[12] A/6695.

In view of the rapid progress in the development of new techniques by technologically advanced countries, it is feared that the situation will change and that the seabed . . . will become progressively and competitively subject to national appropriation and use. This is likely to result in the militarization of the accessible ocean floor through the establishment of fixed military installations and in the exploitation and depletion of resources of immense potential benefit to the world, for the national advantage of technologically developed countries.

Therefore, the Maltese government considered that the time has come to declare the seabed and the ocean floor a common heritage of mankind and that immediate steps should be taken to draft a treaty embodying, *inter alia*, the following principles:

(a) The seabed and the ocean floor, underlying the seas beyond the limits of present national jurisdiction, are not subject to national appropriation in any manner whatsoever;

(b) The exploration of the seabed and of the ocean floor, underlying the seas beyond the limits of present national jurisdiction, shall be undertaken in a manner consistent with the Principles and Purposes of the Charter of the United Nations;

(c) The use of the seabed and the ocean floor, underlying the seas beyond the limits of present national jurisdiction, and their economic exploitation shall be undertaken with the aim of safeguarding the interests of mankind. The net financial benefits derived from the use and exploitation of the seabed and of the ocean floor shall be used primarily to promote the development of poor countries;

(d) The seabed and the ocean floor, underlying the seas beyond the limits of present national jurisdiction, shall be reserved exclusively for peaceful purposes in perpetuity.

The Maltese proposal would also create an international agency:

(i) to assume jurisdiction, as a trustee for all countries, over the seabed and the ocean floor, underlying the seas beyond the limits of present national jurisdiction;

(ii) to regulate, supervise and control all activities thereon; and

(iii) to ensure that the activities undertaken conform to the principles of the provisions of the proposed treaty.

The Maltese proposal was placed on the General Assembly's agenda and sent to the First Committee for consideration.[13] As a result of Committee debates the General Assembly adopted on December 18, 1967, Resolution 2340 (XXII), which established an *ad hoc*, thirty-five member committee to "study the scope and various aspects of this item" and to report to the General Assembly on such topics as

(a) A survey of the past and present activities of the United Nations, the specialized agencies, the International Atomic Energy Agency and other inter-governmental parties with regard to the seabed and the ocean floor and of existing international agreements concerning these areas;

(b) An account of the scientific, technical, economic, legal and other aspects of this item;

(c) An indication regarding practical means to promote international co-operation in the exploitation, conservation and use of the seabed and the ocean floor, and the subsoil thereof, as contemplated in the title of the item, and of their resources, having regard to the views expressed and the suggestions put forward by member states during the consideration of this item at the Twenty-Second Session of the General Assembly.

The resolution further requested the Secretary-General to render all appropriate assistance to the *Ad Hoc* Committee, including the submission of the results of the studies previously noted, and of such other documentation as may be provided by

---

[13] The First Committee is the General Assembly's principal committee for political and security problems. The fact that the proposal was sent to the First Committee, as opposed to the Second Committee, which normally considers economic problems and did, in fact, consider the resolution on the "Resources of the Sea," indicates the perceived importance of this problem.

the various intergovernmental bodies and specialized agencies that had been invited to cooperate.

The preamble of the Resolution 2340 mentions the principal points of interest in the handling of the problems concerned: maintaining international peace and security, exploitation and use of the respective areas for the benefit of all mankind, prohibition of actions and uses which might be detrimental to the common interest of mankind, international cooperation and coordination in the further peaceful exploration and use.

The title of Resolution 2340, modifying the title of the item introduced by the Government of Malta, indicated the two points of the present concern of the General Assembly and serves as guidance for the work of the *Ad Hoc* Committee and of all other organs and agencies cooperating in the work. First, is a desire to maintain international peace and security. Thus, the seabed and subsoil beyond the present limits of national jurisdiction should be exclusively reserved for peaceful purposes. This means that no military installations may be established there. Second, the resources of the submarine area should be used in the interest of mankind. During the Committee debates many speakers suggested that this could be best effected by using the newly accessible resources, principally, to assist developing countries. An important corollary of this concern that the Committee also considered is the prohibition of all uses detrimental to the benefit of mankind.

## Other Proposals

The *Ad Hoc* Committee established by the General Assembly held three meetings, working in groups dealing with economic and technical questions, and with legal questions. In the course of its work, the Committee discussed all aspects of the agenda item. Proposals were submitted by several delegations, including draft resolutions concerning general principles and the prohibition of the use of the seabed for military purposes. The final report submitted to the General Assembly [14] contains an extensive review of technical, economic, and legal problems, but does not propose any of the texts suggested by various delegations. They are simply listed and reproduced either in an annex or in the text of the report itself. There are two sets of proposals: one concerning a declaration or statement of general principles governing the submarine areas beyond the limits of present national jurisdiction,[15] the other concerning the question of disarmament or limitation of armaments.[16]

A proposal concerning the International Decade of Ocean Exploration and another dealing with the danger of sea pollution were also submitted and found wide support. It was felt that a precise delimitation of the area was needed, but discussion on that point was barred by the view of several delegations that it went beyond the Committee's terms of reference. Finally, a Belgian proposal aimed at the establishment of a standing committee to continue the study of all questions involved.

The *Ad Hoc* Committee's report and the entire question of the uses of the seabed were extensively discussed in the First Committee of the General Assembly during its Twenty-Third Session. The First Committee devoted a long series of meetings to a discussion of the various aspects of the matter. The opinions expressed in the proceedings of the *Ad Hoc* Committee were developed and new views added. Almost all delegations participated in the work on that item. As a result, on December 21, 1968, four resolutions—2467 (XXIII) A, B, C, and D—were adopted. None of the aforementioned proposals or draft resolutions except the Belgian proposal to establish a standing committee was accepted. For the rest, the General Assembly wished to

---

[14] A/7230.  [15] A/AC.135/21, 25 and 36.

[16] A/AC.135/20, 24, 26, and 27. See *infra*, p. 148–56.

continue the study of all aspects of the item, and invited the standing committee and other organizations and bodies involved to contribute to the study and to cooperate therein.

Resolution A established a Committee on the Peaceful Uses of the Seabed and Ocean Floor beyond the Limits of National Jurisdiction (hereinafter called the Seabed Committee), and instructed it to study different aspects connected with the matter in close cooperation with bodies dealing with the respective problems, requesting it to submit reports on its activities at each subsequent session of the General Assembly, and to make recommendations on the questions involved. Resolution B requested the Secretary-General to undertake a study of measures that may be taken to protect against possible pollution arising from exploration and exploitation of the seabed and ocean floor.

Resolution C requested the Secretary-General to undertake a study on the question of the establishment of international machinery for the promotion of the exploration and exploitation of the resources of this area, and the use of these resources in the interests of mankind. Resolution D welcomed the concept of an International Decade of Ocean Exploration and invited the member states, the International Oceanographic Commission, and the Secretary-General to cooperate with each other in this respect. In view of the considerable interest many countries had shown for the problem, the Seabed Committee was enlarged to 42 members. Further, it was agreed that, in principle, one third of the membership would rotate every two years. There is, however, no formal provision to that effect, but it is expected that informal arrangements will be worked out by regional groups. Finally, any state wishing to follow the work of the Committee is entitled to accredited observer status. In the first year, sixteen states availed themselves of that provision and were represented by observers.[17]

---

[17] *Report of the Committee on the Peaceful Uses of the Seabed and the Ocean Floor Beyond the Limits of National Jurisdiction*, U.N. Doc. A/7622

The Seabed Committee worked during 1969 on the same pattern as its predecessor. The Economic and Technical Sub-Committee gave detailed consideration to the ways and means of promoting the exploitation and use of the resources of the concerned area and to a long-term program of oceanic exploration. The Legal Sub-Committee made some progress in formulating a set of principles and hoped to continue these efforts during future sessions. The Committee was not able at that stage to make any specific recommendations on substantive matters.

The Report of the Seabed Committee was the object of ample discussion in the General Assembly's First Committee. As a result, the General Assembly adopted four resolutions—2574 A, B, C, and D (XXIV)—dealing with different aspects of the subject. In Resolution 2574 A, the General Assembly stated that there exists an area of the seabed and ocean floor and the subsoil thereof which lies beyond the limits of national jurisdiction; that this area should be used exclusively for peaceful purposes and its resources utilized for the benefit of all mankind; that it must be preserved from encroachment, or appropriation by any state; and that the establishment of an equitable régime for this area would facilitate the task of determining the limits of the area to which that régime is to apply. Therefore, the General Assembly requested the Secretary-General "to ascertain the views of Member States on the desirability of convening at an

---

(1969), p. 3, note 2 (hereinafter cited as *Report of the Seabed Committee*). The agreement on rotation in two-year periods as well as the results of the Committee's work in the first year of its activity indicate that the study of the problem will last several years and no definite results may be expected in the very near future. By contrast, the debates in the General Assembly during its Twenty-Fourth Session show the desire of a majority of states (opposed in a certain manner by the principal major states) to arrive at a solution in a shorter time. Nevertheless, the discussion of all questions mentioned in the resolutions of the General Assembly voted in December, 1969—see especially the program of consultations in Resolution 2574 A (XXIV)—requires a long time, and final solutions cannot be expected before a couple of years.

early date a conference on the law of the sea to review the régimes of the high seas, the continental shelf, the territorial sea and contiguous zone, fishing and conservation of the living resources of the high seas, particularly in order to arrive at a clear, precise and internationally accepted definition of the area of the sea-bed and ocean floor which lies beyond the limits of national jurisdiction, in the light of the international régime to be established for that area." A report on the result of these consultations was requested for submission to the General Assembly at its Twenty-Fifth Session.

By this resolution the General Assembly outlined the future development of its work and of the future legal order. The affirmation of the existence of an area beyond the limits of national jurisdiction indicated the wish of the majority of the United Nations members to constitute an area to be submitted, as the resolution further pronounces, to an international régime and to be utilized for the benefit of all mankind. Taking into account that deeper parts of the ocean bed and subsoil will, for a long time, be practically unusable, because economically not exploitable, the limits of that area should not be put at an excessively deep point.

By Resolution 2574 B the General Assembly invited the Seabed Committee to continue its work, and especially to formulate principles designed to promote international cooperation in the exploration and use of the seabed and subsoil, and to submit a draft declaration of these principles. Equally, the Committee was requested to formulate recommendations regarding the economic and technical conditions of the rules for the exploitation of the resources of the envisaged area. Here again, the wish of the majority of the members points to the conclusion that they wish to constitute an area where exploitation is both technically possible and economically rewarding.

The scope of Resolutions 2574 C and D is set forth below. Before the introduction of the Maltese proposal, various countries had undertaken research studies on the technological, economic and legal problems associated with exploiting and using the ocean depths. The Maltese proposal, however, has had an impact on the problem and has inspired discussion and many studies. The experience of the United States is illustrative. After the Maltese proposal over twenty resolutions were introduced before the United States Congress. All but one of these opposed the idea of vesting control of deep sea resources in an international body. This view was also shared by the House Subcommittee on International Organizations and Movements which, after hearings, reported that it

believed that it would be precipitate, unwise, and possibly injurious to the objectives which both the United States and the United Nations have in common, to reach a decision at this time on a matter which vitally affects the welfare of future generations.[18]

Positive reaction to the internationalization of the ocean's depth has been expressed by Senator Claiborne Pell of Rhode Island. Senator Pell, who has recently considered many of the relevant problems in his book *Challenge of the Seven Seas* (1966), has introduced a resolution to the United States Senate calling for the United States to sponsor a draft declaration in the United Nations General Assembly, which proposes that:

1. the legal concept of the continental shelf be redefined so that the sovereign rights of coastal states can extend no further than the six hundred meter isobath;
2. all ocean space beyond the six hundred meter isobath be free from national appropriation;
3. all unclaimable ocean space and the resources found therein be opened to exploitation by all nations;
4. such exploitation be regulated by a licensing authority designed by the United Nations;

---

[18] *House Comm. on Foreign Affairs, Interim Report on the United Nations and the Issue of Deep Ocean Resources,* House Report No. 999, 90th Congress, 1st Sess., 1967, at 4R.

5. seabed and subsoil not subject to national appropriation only be used for peaceful purposes; and

6. the United Nations establish a sea guard to promote the objectives and ensure the observance of the above items.[19]

## Some Critical Comments on the Maltese and Related Proposals: The Disarmament Problem

In this part of the study we will deal with some of the ideas advocated in the recent proposals and during the debates in the United Nations: utilization of the deep ocean space for peaceful purposes only, the earmarking of its resources for the benefit of all mankind, and the establishment of an international regime.

The reservation for exclusively peaceful purposes implies

---

[19] S. Res. 186, November 17, 1967, 90th Congress, 1st Sess., *Congressional Record*, vol. 113, p. 33020. See also S. Res. 172, *ibid.*, at p. 27322 (Sept. 29, 1967), also proposed by Senator Pell. On March 5, 1968, Senator Pell proposed a draft "Ocean Space Treaty" along the same lines as the proposal contained in S. Res. 186. S. Res. 263, 90th Cong., 2nd Sess., *ibid.*, vol. 114, p. 5181. A new text on the same lines was proposed by Senator Pell in January, 1969, in the form of a Declaration to be adopted by the U.N. General Assembly. S. Res. 33, 91st Congress, 1st Sess., *ibid.*, vol. 115, p. 1330.

Various unofficial International Organizations have also considered aspects of the problem. For example, the International Law Association has issued a preliminary report which, after recognizing that advancing technology may soon make possible recovery of natural resources found at great depths, and that such exploitation must be regulated, suggested that control be vested in an international body which shall govern according to international law. Consideration of the problem has also been undertaken by the World Peace Through Law Center and the Commission to Study the Organization of Peace, the research affiliate of the United Nations Association of the United States. Both organizations would entrust the United Nations with jurisdiction and control over the resources of the deep seas. Further, the Yugoslav Association for Maritime Law, the Yugoslav Association for International Law, and a joint research group composed of members of the Adriatic Institute of Zagreb and the Institute for International Law and International Relations in Zagreb have examined various problems relating to the continental shelf and the exploitation of the natural resources found thereon. See Andrassy, "Potreba Dalje Kodifikacije Medjunarodnog Prava Mora" ("The Necessity for a New Codification of the International Law of the Sea"), *Jugoslovenska Revija za Medjunarodno Pravo (Yugoslav Review for International Law)*, 1965, No. 2.

the prohibition of military uses. In the recent past there have been some instances of international agreements directing the contracting parties to abstain from using determined areas or spaces for military purposes. There are also suggestions to prohibit the deployment or use of certain weapons in determined areas or regions.

The Antarctic Treaty, signed at Washington on December 1, 1955,[20] declares that Antarctica shall be used for peaceful purposes only, and that any measures of a military nature shall be prohibited.

Another important text relates to outer space. By Resolution 1348 (XIII) the General Assembly [21] established an *Ad Hoc* Committee on the Peaceful Uses of Outer Space and adopted some guiding principles for the uses of outer space (1958). The final result of the work of the *Ad Hoc* Committee and of long negotiations was Resolution 2222 (XXI) by which the General Assembly adopted the text of the Treaty on Principles Governing the Activities of States in the Exploration and Use of Outer Space (1966).[22] Among other important provisions the treaty prohibits the placing in orbit around the Earth of any objects carrying nuclear weapons or any other kinds of weapons of mass destruction, the installation of such weapons on celestial bodies, and the stationing of such weapons in outer space in any other manner. The moon and other celestial bodies shall be used exclusively for peaceful purposes.

Since the proposal for a nuclear-free zone in Europe by the Polish Minister of Foreign Affairs Adam Rapacki (1957), several attempts have been made in order to assure at least regional

---

[20] *United Nations Treaty Series*, vol. 402, p. 71.

[21] Between 1958 and 1966 several resolutions of the General Assembly on the same subject, including Resolution 1962 (XVIII) containing a Declaration of Legal Principles Governing the Activities of States in the Exploration and Use of Outer Space (1963), were adopted.

[22] *United States Treaties and Other International Agreements*, vol. 18, p. 2410. *United Nations Treaty Series*, vol. 634.

zones where the production, stationing and use of nuclear weapons would be prohibited. This is the aim of a treaty [23] signed at Mexico City on February 14, 1967, at a conference of Latin American States prohibiting the use of nuclear energy and of nuclear installations for other than peaceful purposes. The parties to the treaty must prohibit on their respective territories any tests, uses, production, and acquisition of nuclear weapons. More limited in scope, but universal with respect to state participation, is the Treaty Banning Nuclear Weapons Tests in the Atmosphere, in Outer Space, and Under Water (August 5, 1963).[24]

The question of prohibiting the use of the ocean space for military purposes is of course linked with the general problem of disarmament. It could therefore be said that it cannot be solved outside the negotiations on disarmament. However, in disarmament negotiations partial solutions can be envisaged and have in fact been brought about by the two aforementioned treaties. These treaties and the projects on nuclear-free zones remove determined areas from specified military uses or even for all military uses. The ocean space too can be the object of a partial disarmament agreement. Moreover, the uses of the seabed and its subsoil for military purposes are new in kind, and they can be specifically determined in such a manner that the traditional uses of the sea for navigation of navy crafts need not be affected.[25] In that way, the immediate goal of the Maltese and similar proposals could be reached outside the general work on disarma-

---

[23] Treaty for the Prohibition of Nuclear Weapons in Latin America, *International Legal Materials,* vol. 6, p. 521–34. A special regional organization implements the treaty. Its organs include a general assembly composed of all parties to the treaty, a council, composed of five members elected by the general assembly for a four-year term, and a secretariat. The secretary-general is nominated by the general assembly.

[24] *United Nations Treaty Series,* vol. 480, p. 43.

[25] On June 20, 1968 the Soviet Government proposed an interdiction of military uses of the seabed for the entire area outside the territorial waters, i.e., including the continental shelf which is inside the limits of present national jurisdiction. See A/AC.135/20.

ment problems. The prohibition could be couched in the form of a declaration of the United Nations General Assembly, or in the form of a treaty framed on the model of the Treaty on Antarctica and the Treaty on the Exploration and Use of Outer Space.

Discussions of the problem of military uses of the seabed and their prohibition or limitation have given rise to some proposals in the *Ad Hoc* Committee, established by General Assembly Resolution 2340 (XXII), and in the Eighteen-Nation Committee on Disarmament. Of course, the two military superpowers presented their proposals, and these proposals may serve as an example for demonstrating the divergences of approach and opinion which will continue and develop in further discussions during the work of the new Seabed Committee, established by General Assembly Resolution 2467 (XXIII), and in the Eighteen-Nation Disarmament Committee.

The first proposal made by the Soviet Union calls upon all states to use the seabed beyond the limits of the territorial waters exclusively for peaceful purposes and requests the Eighteen-Nation Disarmament Committee to consider as an urgent matter the question of prohibiting the use for military purposes of the seabed beyond the limits of the territorial waters.[26]

The next proposal was made in the *Ad Hoc* Committee by the United States. After indicating a desire that workable arms limitation measures be achieved, which will enhance the peace and security of all nations and bring the world nearer to general and complete disarmament, the operative part of the proposed draft resolution requested the Eighteen-Nation Disarmament Committee to take up the question of arms limitation on the seabed with a view to defining those factors vital to a workable, verifiable, and effective international agreement which would prevent the use of this new environment for the emplacement of weapons of mass destruction.[27]

[26] *Ibid.*                    [27] June 28, 1968, A/AC.135/24.

A third proposal was submitted by Tanzania in the form of amendments to the proposals of the Soviet Union and the United States. It proposes a declaration "that the sea-bed and the ocean floor and the subsoil thereof, underlying the high seas beyond present national jurisdiction, should not be used by any State or States for any military purposes whatsoever," and requests the Eighteen-Nation Disarmament Committee "to consider, as a matter of urgency, the question of (a) banning the use of the sea-bed and ocean floor beyond the limits of national jurisdiction by nuclear submarines; (b) banning of military fortifications and missile bases on the sea-bed and ocean floor." [28]

Comparing these three proposals, it is apparent that the two superpowers are in favor of exclusively peaceful uses of the seabed of the high seas, but they do not consider the barring of these areas for military use to be a principle of existing international law. The prohibition of military uses should be reached by negotiations within the framework of the general United Nations work on disarmament. Tanzania's proposal, however, calls at least for a declaration of principle prohibiting the use of the seabed for military purposes. Nevertheless, Tanzania does accept the need to discuss the prohibition of various kinds of arms by the special organ for disarmament questions and urges the banning of nuclear submarines, military fortifications, and missile bases on the ocean floor.

Thus, the international community is faced with the fact that the prohibition of military uses of the seabed must be negotiated and reached by international negotiations and agreement instead of initially being declared to be a principle. Here, the proposals of the two superpowers differ on two principal points. First, although the Soviet proposal aims at a complete prohibition of all military uses, the United States proposal refers to the interdiction of arms of mass destruction only. Second, the Soviet

---

[28] July 2, 1968, A/AC.135/26 and 27.

proposal extends the prohibition to all submarine areas under the high seas, including the continental shelf region in which coastal states enjoy certain "sovereign rights." Both powers maintained their views and proposals during the March–April, 1969 meeting of the Eighteen-Nation Disarmament Committee. President Nixon reaffirmed, in a letter,[29] the wish that the seabed remain free from the nuclear arms race and advocated the negotiation of an international agreement that would prohibit placing nuclear weapons or other weapons of mass destruction on the seabed. The Soviet Union, however, presented a draft treaty on prohibition on the use of the seabed for military purposes, and the ocean floor and the subsoil thereof, wherein the prohibited area is more precisely defined. It encompasses the seabed and subsoil beyond a 12-mile maritime zone measured from the baselines as they are used to define the limits of the territorial waters. The Soviet proposal adheres to the rule of Article 24 of the Convention on the Territorial Sea. Free access to all installations and structures of the seabed will permit verification as to whether states which have placed such objects thereon have fulfilled the obligations assumed under the proposed treaty.[30]

Halfway between the United States and Soviet view are the suggestions submitted to the Eighteen-Nation Disarmament Committee by Canada. Canada proposed that the largest possible area should be reserved for peaceful purposes, but this should not preclude its use for purely defensive purposes in a zone adjacent to the coast. This defensive zone would extend some 200 miles beyond the outer limits of the 12-mile belt as proposed by the Soviet Union. While supporting the United States proposal to prohibit the emplacement of nuclear and other weapons of mass destruction, Canada suggested that the prohibition should, in addition, cover all other weapons, military activities, undersea

---

[29] Published as an official document, March 18, 1969, ENDC/239.
[30] March 18, 1969, ENDC/240.

bases and fortifications from which military action could be undertaken against the territory, territorial sea, or air space of another state.

After prolonged debate in the Eighteen-Nation Committee on Disarmament, and on the basis of additional negotiations, the Soviet Union and the United States submitted to the committee a draft treaty [31] that limited the prohibition to "any objects with nuclear weapons or any other types of weapons of mass destruction, as well as structures, launching installations or any other facilities specifically designed for storing, testing and using such weapons." The prohibited zone encompasses "the seabed and the ocean floor and the subsoil thereof beyond the maximum contiguous zone provided for in the 1958 Geneva Convention on the Territorial Sea and the Contiguous Zone." The outer limit of the said contiguous zone "shall be measured in accordance with the provisions of Part I, Section II of the 1958 Geneva Convention on the Territorial Sea and the Contiguous Zone and in accordance with international law." But in view of the fact that all states have not yet extended their territorial sea to the maximum width as laid down in the said Convention, there would be offshore such states a zone not covered by the prohibition where the principle of the freedom of the seas would allow the emplacement of prohibited weapons. This gap is covered by a provision of the draft treaty saying that the prohibition of emplantation and emplacement extends to these zones too, except that they shall not apply to the coastal state. In this way a new special zone off the coasts would be created. Its extension would be uniform for all states. The coastal state alone would be authorized to use this zone for any military purposes. A further consequence of that provision is that each coastal state, having a territorial sea of less than 12 miles, would have the right of inspection and control over a part of the sea out-

---

[31] The draft treaty and all preceding proposals are reproduced in *Report of the Conference of the Committee on Disarmament*, U.N. Doc. A/7741.

side the limits of its territorial sea in order to prohibit or prevent the emplantation or emplacement of prohibited weapons in that zone. A right of individual or joint verification is recognized to all contracting parties in order to ensure the observance of the provisions of the treaty.

The text of the draft treaty was approved by the Conference of the Committee on Disarmament [32] and annexed to its report to the General Assembly. By Resolution 2602 F (XXIV) the General Assembly took note of the report and the annexed draft treaty, welcomed it, and called upon the Conference of the Committee on Disarmament "to take into account all proposals and suggestions that have been made at this session of the General Assembly and to continue its work on this subject so that the text of a draft treaty can be submitted to the General Assembly for its consideration." [33]

In this way, an important step was made towards a partial elimination of the arms race with respect to the seabed of the high seas and its subsoil. Certainly, the present text of the draft treaty will be modified in view of the many observations made in the General Assembly's First Committee, but it can be expected that a treaty on the lines of the present draft could be submitted for signature at the end of 1970 or 1971. Of course, the ultimate aim should be to prohibit the use of the seabed of the high seas and its subsoil for all military purposes. This aim cannot be attained but by long negotiations in the framework of general and complete disarmament. However, it is possible that the special question of the military uses of the seabed and its subsoil may become a separate item and represent a step

---

[32] In the summer of 1969 the Eighteen-Nation Disarmament Committee was enlarged by eight new members and it was decided to change its name to the "Committee on Disarmament," and the name of the Conference to "Conference of the Committee on Disarmament." This was endorsed by G. A. Res. 2602 B (XXIV).

[33] See, in this respect, *Report of the First Committee: Questions of General and Complete Disarmament,* U.N. Doc. A/7902, and the documents cited in para. 6.

toward general disarmament. In this respect, it is important to recall that it is absolutely necessary that all major military powers become parties to such an agreement. Generally speaking, the United Nations organs are appropriate for discussion and agreement, but the absence of the People's Republic of China representation therein is an important stumbling block to success.

This is true not only from the purely technical aspect since an agreement on disarmament, even partial, is closely linked to, and depends on, the solution of several major political questions. Any delay will bring new difficulties because of the quick pace of progress in the construction of weapons and military installations in submarine areas.

Finally, as observed at the Twenty-Third Session of the General Assembly, the demilitarization problem cannot be disassociated from the whole question concerning the regime and the uses of the seabed.[34]

## Exploitation for the Benefit of Mankind

The use and exploitation of ocean space shall safeguard the interests of mankind, and the benefit from the use and exploitation primarily shall be employed to promote the development of poor countries. This guiding principle requires detailed elaboration by a deliberative body and an executive organ which will apply the directives received and supervise the activities in the ocean space. This point will be discussed in the next section of the present chapter.

The principle that the ocean space shall be used and exploited in a manner safeguarding the interests of mankind is designed to counter the danger that various uses and exploitation methods might unduly deplete the natural resources without giv-

[34] See the declaration of the French delegate at the 1591st meeting of the General Assembly's First Committee, October 30, 1968, A/C.1/PV. 1591.

ing to mankind all the possible benefits of more rational uses. For this very reason it is necessary that an appropriate and efficient authority be established to take care of the interests of mankind, present and future, in the uses and exploitation of the ocean space.

## *An International Agency for the Control of Seabed Uses and Other Proposals*

The Maltese memorandum proposes the establishment of an international agency which will have jurisdiction over the ocean space, will regulate and supervise all activities, and ensure that they conform to the principles and provisions which might be applicable.

In proposing that vast submarine areas outside the present national jurisdiction shall be declared a common heritage of mankind, not subject to any national appropriation, and that the national resources therein shall be exploited with the aim of safeguarding the interests of mankind, Malta envisaged the creation of an international agency with the task:

(a) to assume jurisdiction, as a trustee for all countries, over the seabed and the ocean floor, underlying the seas beyond the limits of present national jurisdiction;

(b) to regulate, supervise and control all activities thereon; and

(c) to ensure that the activities undertaken conform to the principles and provisions of the proposed treaty.

Although the Maltese proposal was favorably received in the General Assembly (in the debates of the First Committee), the proposal to establish an international agency has found but few supporters. Ghana, Sweden, Japan, and Iran were in favor of the idea. The proposal presupposes, however, an agreement on cooperation in the exploitation of natural resources of submarine areas. The delegate of Sierra Leone was also in favor of some form of international jurisdiction and control. Liberia wished to institute an international consortium as a machinery for exploring and exploiting the natural resources of the seabed and ocean floor for the benefit of mankind.

Some other delegates sought to postpone the decision about an international regime until a later date. Turkey sponsored the creation of a study committee and expressed its support for the plan to place the ocean depth under United Nations jurisdiction. The Swedish delegate, Mrs. A. Myrdal, considered an international supervisory and regulatory regime indispensable. Such an agency should be able to assume a variety of functions. The Swedish delegate proposed that internationalization should be mentioned in the proposed resolution of the General Assembly as the ultimate goal.

General Assembly Resolution 2340 (XXII) did not ask the *Ad Hoc* Committee to study that question. The following year, at the urging of some delegations during the Twenty-Third Session of the General Assembly, the General Assembly adopted Resolution 2467 C (XXIII) which requested that the Secretary-General undertake a study on the question of establishing appropriate international machinery for the promotion of the exploration and exploitation of the resources of the deep submarine area, and the use of these resources in the interests of mankind.[35]

While parts A, B, and D were adopted without opposition, Resolution 2467 C met with strong opposition from the Soviet

---

[35] The Secretary-General prepared an extensive study of the question of establishing an international machinery. See *Study on the question of establishing in due time appropriate international machinery for the promotion of exploration and exploitation of the resources of the sea-bed and the ocean floor beyond the limits of national jurisdiction, and the use of these resources in the interests of mankind*, U.N. Doc. A/AC.138/12, reprinted in *Report of the Seabed Committee, supra* note 17, at p. 81. The Seabed Committee had insufficient time to study the question during its 1969 meetings, although its Economic and Technical Sub-Committee made some observations on the question. The Committee proposed that the Secretary-General continue the study in depth, and the General Assembly adopted this proposal and requested the Committee to prepare a report for the 1970 session.

Union and Eastern European states who voted against its adoption, and a cool attitude on the part of the three Western great powers and half of the Western developed countries (which abstained). A great majority of developing countries supported the resolution; they were joined by several developed countries and by Yugoslavia. The resolution was carried by a vote of eighty-five to nine, with twenty-five abstentions.

## Characteristics of Agency for an International Régime

We now turn to the question of how to organize the authority responsible for uses of the seabed and subsoil of the ocean space, and the exploitation of their natural resources, and the first point is whether an existing international organization or a new agency should be entrusted with this task. In this respect we should be guided by the idea that the ocean space and its resources are or should be proclaimed the common heritage of mankind. Consequently, all states should participate in the agency concerned.

Although the United Nations, as well as its specialized agencies, aspire to be universal, none of them are. Moreover, their statutes contain provisions on admission and exclusion of members which make it possible that some states are denied, or excluded from, membership. Finally, the distribution of responsibilities and tasks among various agencies permits every state to participate in one or the other of the agencies and to keep out of others in which it does not wish to participate. If we keep in mind that the tasks and responsibilities concerning the ocean space and its natural resources are fairly extensive and have a special character, the establishment of a separate new agency might appear as justified. There are, however, forms and possibilities of having a separate lateral organization in the framework of an existing organization. UNCTAD and some other organizations were established on that pattern. A more simple machinery could be created by establishing a special service or center within the United Nations Secretariat.[36] Of course, in such a case, the attributes of such a machinery would be more modest.

The following considerations envisage the establishment of such a new agency responsible for ocean space affairs, but they might be useful also in case an existing organization (the United Nations or another) may be entrusted with the task.

(1) *Membership.* The membership in the agency should be open to all nations, as is appropriate for an organization responsible for a "common heritage of mankind." The universality of the agency should be improved in comparison with the existing international organization where admission and exclusion of members exist. True universality cannot be attained if there is no automatic admission to membership of all existing states. However, there cannot be an obligation to become a member. Therefore a formal application should be made declaring the willingness of the applicant state to become a member and to assume the obligations imposed by the statute and other rules governing the activity of the agency.

The responsible organ should only register the application and notify the entry of the new member to other members. The application may be dismissed if the responsible organ considers that the applicant does not qualify as a state. This could happen for example, if the following were to apply for admission: a territorial or other unit not having the quality of a state, a member of a federal state having no separate international personality, or a rival government which does not exercise any effective authority over the territory it claims. But the unsuccessful applicant should have the opportunity to seek redress. The International

---

[36] Examples are given in the report of the Secretary-General, *supra* note 35, at pp. 121–22.

Court of Justice might be asked to decide whether the applicant is or is not a state eligible for membership. If the decision is in the affirmative, the applicant must be registered. Every member of the agency should be given the right to question the eligibility of an applicant for admission and to refer the question to the Court.

The universality of the organization does not tolerate the procedure of a formal exclusion. Members acting against the rules or aims of the organization could only be suspended from the exercise of their rights and/or from the sharing of the benefits. However, the organization cannot be compulsory. Therefore, members should have the right to withdraw from membership. In that case, the member state would lose rights acquired during the period of his membership.

(2) *Organs.* The normal pattern of similar agencies shows a three-tier organizational structure. There are usually three principal organs: an assembly of all members, as the policy-making organ; a board or council having a restricted number of members and exercising certain administrative, executive, and supervisory functions; a director or secretary-general as the chief executive organ. This general pattern may undergo various modifications corresponding to the needs of the respective tasks and to the views of the founding members.

In the case of an agency dealing with ocean space matters, there will be a large number of administrative and executive tasks which demand quick and definite solutions. Thus, the administrative and executive organ should be able to make decisions. Having in mind the extensive functions of the respective organ with respect to ocean space and its resources, some projects propose that the organ at this level should not be one individual person but a board or council composed of several persons in their individual capacity. The project of the Center for the Study of Democratic Institutions proposes such a body (commission) composed of individuals chosen on the basis of their competence only, responsible to the assembly of the organization, and independent of any influence by the governments of their respective states. An analogous organ is established in the European Communities. Bodies composed of personalities not representing their states are to be found also in some specialized agencies, although not on the executive level.

In view of the special task of the agency, much could be said in favor of a scheme where the policy-making organ would have a composition different from the ordinary one-state-one-vote pattern. The great number of tiny states in the United Nations itself has prompted discussions on the advisability of introducing a weighted voting system. Weighted voting has been introduced in some organizations, especially in the European Communities, but not on the most important level. Another pattern has been found in some commodity agreements seeking a balance between groups of members with opposite, but complementary interests. Whether there could be an alternative to the ordinary pattern, as expressed in the composition of the United Nations General Assembly, cannot be answered without knowing more specifically the responsibilities and powers of the agency and of its organs. In the opinion of the present author, an assembly of all members, everyone having one vote, could not be a very appropriate organ for taking binding decisions.

For such an organ with a more restricted membership, different models could be considered. In all cases the distribution of seats should reflect geographical regions as well as different interest groups. As examples we shall consider the composition of the respective organs of the United Nations Industrial Development Organizaton (UNIDO) and of the United Nations Development Program.

THE UNIDO MODEL. The United Nations Industrial Development Organization has been established as an organ of the General Assembly functioning as an autonomous organization of the United Nations.[37] The principal organ of the organization is the Industrial Development Board, which consists of forty-five members elected by the General Assembly for a term of three years; every year a third of the members are elected. The members of the board are chosen from among the states members of the United Nations, members of the specialized agencies, and the International Atomic Energy Agency. The seats are distributed on the basis of a special scheme having due regard to the principle of equitable geographical representation. The scheme sets up four groups of states. Two groups are determined by regional criteria, two other groups by the stage of development. In the first group are sixty-eight developing countries to which are allotted eighteen seats. From the second group (thirty developed countries and the Holy See) fifteen members are to be elected, from the third group (twenty-three Latin American states) seven members, and from the fourth group (nine Eastern European states) five members.[38]

THE ORGANIZATION OF THE UNITED NATIONS DEVELOPMENT PROGRAM. A complicated formula is used in Resolution 2029 (XX) of the United Nations General Assembly concerning the United Nations Development Program. The Governing Council of that program shall be elected by the Economic and Social Council

from among States Members of the United Nations or members of the specialized agencies or of the International Atomic Energy Agency, providing for equitable and balanced representation of the economically more developed countries, on the one hand, having due regard to their contribution to the United Nations Develop-

---

[37] The organization was established in 1965 by General Assembly Resolution 2089 (XX) and its statute was adopted by Resolution 2152 (XXI).

[38] The lists of the four groups shall be reviewed by the board in the light of changes in the membership. However, new additions to the lists were made by General Assembly resolutions. By the end of 1969, the group of developing countries included 72, the Latin American group 24 states. Resolution 2570 (XXIV).

ment Programme, and of the developing countries, on the other hand, taking into account the need for suitable regional representation among the latter members and in accordance with the provisions of the annex to the present resolution. . . .

The said annex provides that nineteen seats in the council shall be filled by developing countries and seventeen seats by economically more developed countries, and in each of the two groups the allocation shall be made by regions as defined in the annex itself.

The developing countries are divided into three groups: Asia, Africa, and Latin America. Yugoslavia is to be added to one of these three groups according to an agreement to be reached among the developing countries. In this group African states are represented by seven members; Asia and Latin America by six members each. Of the seventeen seats allocated to the economically more developed countries, fourteen shall be filled by Western European and "other" countries and three by Eastern European countries. The term "other" covers all the more developed countries outside Europe. The thirty-seventh seat is the object of a most complicated disposition. It has to be filled in accordance with a nine-year cycle where the three groups of developing countries fill the seat for one year each, and the two groups of more developed countries for three years each.

ORGANIZATIONAL PATTERNS OF COMMODITY AGREEMENTS. Another pattern is used in some commodity agreements, but with the difference that it applies to the composition of the basic policy-making organ. In the case of these agreements there are two distinct groups with complementary interests, and the respective agreements adopt a scheme where each group has an equal number of votes distributed among the members of the respective group. This distribution is made on the basis of the importance of participation of a member in the transactions which are covered by the agreement in question. The International

Coffee Organization, for instance, has as its highest authority the International Coffee Council, composed of all states members of the organization. The members are divided into two categories: exporting and importing countries. Each of the two groups disposes of 1,000 votes which are distributed among the members of the group in the following way:

(a) Each member has five basic votes, but the total number of these votes shall not exceed 150. Therefore, if there are more than thirty members in either group, the number of basic votes shall be adjusted so as to keep the total number of basic votes within the maximum of 150.

(b) In the group of importing countries the remaining votes (850 or a little more) are distributed among the members of the group in proportion to their respective basic export quotas.

(c) In the group of importing countries the remaining votes are distributed among the members of the group in proportion to the average volume of their respective imports in the preceding three-year period.

The distribution of votes is determined by the Council at the beginning of each coffee year. A redistribution shall be made in any case of change in the membership, including the suspension, or the return, of voting rights.

The normal pattern for the executive organ is a monocratic system. The director or secretary-general of the organization is elected or nominated by the policy-making organ or by the council, or by both. He is responsible for the work of the secretariat, which is working under his orders.

THE PROPOSAL OF THE CENTER FOR THE STUDY OF DEMOCRATIC INSTITUTIONS. An interesting and original approach has been offered by the Center for the Study of Democratic Institutions at Santa Barbara.[39] The draft proposes a separate organization combining economic efficiency with political responsibility. Most original is the composition of its two principal organs: the Maritime Commission and the Maritime Assembly. The Maritime Commission would be composed of seventeen members serving for three years. Representatives of five member states most advanced in ocean-space technology would be designated by the outgoing Commission. Twelve members would be elected by the Maritime Assembly, with due regard to equitable representation on the Commission as a whole, namely of developed and developing nations, maritime and landlocked nations, and nations operating under free-enterprise and socialistic economic systems. Any member state not represented on the Commission would appoint an *ad hoc* member whenever its own vital interests are directly concerned; but the number of *ad hoc* members at any time would be limited to four.

The Maritime Assembly, meeting in regular annual and in special sessions, would consist of four chambers of eighty-eight delegates each. The delegates would serve in their personal capacity for three years, and a third would be renewed each year. The first chamber would be elected by the General Assembly of the United Nations: nine members from nine regions of the world. The second chamber would represent international mining corporations, organizations, unions, producers, and consumers directly interested in the extraction of the resources from the seabed and below the seabed. The third chamber would represent fishing organizations, fish processors and merchants, unions of seamen serving on fishing vessels, as well as representatives of such organizations as various fishery commissions (International Whaling Commission and others). The fourth chamber would represent scientists in oceanography, marine biology, meteorol-

---

[39] Borgese, *The Ocean Regime: A Suggested Statute for Peaceful Uses of the High Seas and of the Sea-Bed Beyond the Limits of National Jurisdiction*, 1968.

ogy, and various other sectors related to the exploration of the seas and the seabed.

The manner of election to the last three chambers would have to be determined, but it is certain that this would require a formulated set of rules concerning the nominating bodies and their functioning. Any of the five bodies would be empowered to make decisions and recommendations. They would become operative when approved by the first chamber—that is, the one of the three other chambers having jurisdiction over the matter —and the commission. The draft also proposes the creation of some more executive and consultative organs and of a Maritime Court.

In the course of time there will be more proposals and suggestions. No definite plan will be proposed here. The structure and organization of the agency will, among others, depend also on the scope of attributions and responsibilities of the agency. In this respect we shall give at the end of our considerations only a short tentative outline of its possible functions.

(3) *Functions.*    (a) Research work: Exploration of various factors, the knowledge of which is important for those who use the sea, both on the surface and in the depths; mapping of the sea bottom and its depths; of surface and underwater currents; of the temperature and salinity on the surface and in various depths, etc. Making these data available for all members of the international community.

(b) Service for member states such as weather forecasting and warning from other risks underwater and on the bottom, services which will be badly needed for communications and for exploration and exploitation work; the establishment of a world-wide marine geodetic system.[40]

---

[40] Burke, "Law and the New Technologies," in Alexander, *The Law of the Sea,* 1967, p. 217, noted that "this network would involve the permanent emplacement of equipment on the ocean floor for locating and identifying

(c) Regulation of all uses of the sea, its bottom, and subsoil, especially in order to avoid interference of one kind of use to the detriment of another: surface and submarine navigation; fisheries; cables; pipelines; surface, underwater, and on-the-bottom installations, moving or stationary, for exploration and exploitation of the natural resources of the sea, of its bed, and its subsoil outside the domain of national jurisdiction (territorial sea and continental shelf as restricted in conformity with the amended or reinterpreted Convention on the Continental Shelf); and location of areas reserved for pollution waste disposal.

(d) With respect to the exploration and exploitation of the natural resources of submarine areas: either simple registering of effectively undertaken works for exploration and/or exploitation, or granting of licenses to that effect, in conformity with regulations set forth by a multilateral international agreement entered into to that effect, or laid down in acts or resolutions of responsible international bodies.

(e) Improvement of existing regulations in international agreements, after appropriate studies and consultations: (i) by initiating and convening of international conferences to that effect and proposing draft regulations; or (ii) by issuing such rules on the basis of an authorization granted to that effect in international agreements.[41]

---

bench marks useful for a variety of purpose." Mourad in *Marine Geodesy,* 1965, p. 6, as quoted by Burke, *ibid.,* observed that "among the activities that would benefit from an ocean geodetic grid system are spacecraft recovery, ocean engineering, open ocean tide measurement, calibration of inertial and electronic navigational systems, and seismic and magnetic mapping. Surface and underwater highways could be established on the basis of such a system. Surveying of ocean farming and mining areas would also be facilitated. The grid system could also be used as a basis for an ocean meteorological network of weather observation stations."

[41] For a more detailed exposition of various possible functions, see report of the Secretary-General, *op. cit. supra* note 35, at pp. 100–17.

# Conclusions

(1) The seabed of deeper and deep seas and its subsoil are rich in natural resources. Their exploitation in ever deeper sea areas will become increasingly possible with the progress of science and technology.

(2) As natural resources in greater depth become exploitable the question of the legal regime of these areas arises.

(3) The provisions of the Convention on the Continental Shelf should not be applied in that case because of the inequalities caused by their application in the delimitation of areas with greater water depths.

(4) A sound interpretation of these provisions does not admit their application beyond a certain limit. The latter is not, however, clearly determined.

(5) A verbal interpretation of the definition of the continental shelf, given in the said convention, could be employed in order to extend the claims of coastal states very far, perhaps even lead to a wholesale partition of the submarine areas of all oceans.

(6) Such a consequence is to be feared because coastal states tend to extend their authority toward the high sea.

(7) Such a consequence could be avoided by an agreement defining in clear terms the extension of the continental shelf.

(8) The exploitation of the natural resources of the rest of submarine areas must be regulated by a form of international regime whose details are to be discussed. Eventually, an international agency should be established.

# Postscript

~~~~~~~~~~~~~~~~~~~~~~~~~~~~~~~~~~~~~~~~~~~~~~~~~~~~~~

THE PRESENT STUDY, COMPLETED AT THE BEGINNING OF 1969, is mainly concerned with the question of the outward limit of the continental shelf and a critical analysis of the exploitability test set forth in Article 1 of the Convention on the Continental Shelf. It seeks to demonstrate the inadmissibility of extended claims to submarine areas on the basis of that provision. In the last two years, however, some new views have been put forward which must be taken into consideration.

In a nutshell, these views claim greatly extended limits for the national jurisdiction over the seabed of the high seas and its subsoil, on the basis of certain geophysical features of these areas and of a new interpretation of the Convention on the Continental Shelf.

The geophysical justification for this approach is the division of the earth's crust into two fundamentally distinct geomorphic units: the ocean basins and the continental platforms. The continental slope and the continental rise are said to belong to the unit whose principal part consists of the continents. It is at the dividing line between the submerged part of the continents and the oceanic basins that, in this view, the boundary of the national jurisdiction should be placed. It is asserted that present conventional and customary international law is in accordance with this view and that coastal states are entitled to claim jurisdiction over the whole extent of the continental margin.[1]

Legal arguments supporting this tendency are contained in an article by Professor R. Y. Jennings,[2] which analyzes the judgment of the International Court of Justice in the *North Sea Continental Shelf Cases*. Quoting some dicta of the judgment, the author asserts, although cautiously, that "the idea of a prolongation of the land domain is the legal foundation of the submerged area of national jurisdiction" and that "this concept relates to the geographical and geological fact."[3] From the wording of the definition in Article 1 of the 1958 Geneva Convention on the Continental Shelf, Professor Jennings concludes that the Convention, like the Court, throws the question of the outer limit of the continental shelf (in its legal sense) back to geography or geology or both.

And both in terms of geology and in terms of geomorphology there would seem to be little room for doubt that the continental slope is just as much a part and a prolongation of the continental land mass as the continental shelf is. For it is not just a question of seabed but a question also of subsoil, *viz.*, of the underlying rock structure. The underlying rock structure of the shelf and slope is identical. . . . [C]onsiderations of geography and geology—to which the law itself looks for guidance—lead to the conclusion that the continental slope and subsoil are part and parcel of that "pro-

---

[1] See, for an ample exposition of the above view, *Petroleum Resources under the Ocean Floor*, published by the National Petroleum Council, Washington, 1969.

[2] Jennings, "The Limits of Continental Shelf Jurisdiction: Some Possible Implications of the North Sea Case Judgment," *Int'l & Comp. L.Q.*, vol. 18 (1969), p. 819.

[3] *Ibid.*, at 826.

longation" of the continent over which the coastal State has exclusive jurisdiction." [4]

The author adds that this *a priori* conclusion is in process of confirmation by state practice. Licenses have been granted for exploration or exploitation in regions of the continental slope, and there have been no protests from other states. As for the continental rise, the author considers that an answer is difficult because "here geology itself speaks with an uncertain voice." The author concludes that "the resources of any area which is 'appurtenant', in the sense of being geomorphologically or geologically a part in physical fact of the land mass, must by general international law be deemed already vested in the coastal State." [5]

In the present author's opinion, this interpretation cannot be accepted. First of all, any sound legal interpretation must take into account the text of the Geneva Convention. This text consecrated the practice which began with the Truman Declaration in 1945. All declarations since then have claimed the continental shelf only, without mentioning the continental slope. The International Law Commission was at all times concerned with the definition of the extent of the continental shelf. The parties to the Convention meant to define the extent of the continental shelf and not of "the natural prolongation of continents." It is to that extent only that the Geneva Convention enacted the developing law, and only in this sense can one say that this is also generally accepted customary law. The limit indicated in Article 1 was also meant to determine the extent of the continental shelf. The 200-meter isobath was chosen as a mechanical means of delimitation for purely technical reasons, and with the understanding that it is an average depth at which the steeper fall-off of the seabed to greater depth occurs. In Chapter 1, the authorities are cited for the choice of this measure as the limit of the continental shelf. For Thoulet the continental

---

[4] *Ibid.*, at 829, 830.          [5] *Ibid.*, at 831.

shelf is "the area of the sea bottom between the coast and the isobath of 200 meters or 100 fathoms." Trumbull states that "for convenience the 100 fathom line is more often used." The said isobath was also appropriate because it is the line used most often in sea maps. We must conclude that in choosing the 200-meter isobath the framers of the Convention wished to determine a uniform limit of the continental shelf. The words of a legal text must be interpreted in their normal meaning. The proposition that the framers meant to say that the term "continental shelf" refers to the "natural prolongation of the land mass of the continents" is therefore untenable.[6]

In the Geneva Convention, the term of "adjacency" should be interpreted as a limiting factor. It may be recalled that the theory of contiguity has served as pretext for many territorial claims, but that it was rejected by internationalists as not being recognized in customary international law.[7]

But if we accept the premise that the right to the continental margin derives from the fact of its being the natural prolongation of the land, an inseparable part of the continent, it may be objected that, in that case, all countries of the continent should have the right to a share, not only those that are situated on the coast. Moreover, the claimants to the submarine areas have in mind the rich resources of the seabed and subsoil. The origin of the sediments, formed over millions of years, is the land from which material is carried by rivers into the sea. It seems inequitable to deny a right to these resources to a country whose rivers contributed to their accumulation, for instance, to Congo

---

[6] Professor Jennings himself concedes that the term "continental shelf" has an importance: "Nevertheless the term is one that has an ordinary technical meaning even though not a very exact one and consequently it is not a purely neutral term wherein any given content can be accommodated. There must in law be a presumption that a term is used in its plain meaning." "General Course on Principles of International Law," *Recueil des Cours*, vol. 121 (1967, II), pp. 324–608, at 395.

[7] See Max Huber's arbitral award in the *Island of Palmas Case, Reports of International Arbitral Awards* (Perm. Ct. Arb. 1911), vol. 2, p. 869.

(Kinshasa), whose share in the submarine areas is almost non-existent. The same may be said in all cases where big rivers carry material into the sea from inland countries and not only from the coastal state.

Another argument against the opinion that by the term "continental shelf" the Geneva Convention meant the natural prolongation of continents may be drawn from the fact that the continental shelf in Article 1 of that Convention refers also to submarine areas around islands. Many of these "shelves" do not belong to the "continental platform" as distinct from the "ocean basins." The islands and island groups in the oceans are the highest elevations of oceanic ridges. Their shelves belong to the other of the two "fundamental units" of the earth's crust. We cannot believe that the Convention attributes to islands another sort of "continental shelf" than that attributed to countries on continents. So we must conclude that the term "continental shelf" cannot be extended so as to include the continental slope and rise. It may also be argued that these islands, being part of the oceanic ridges, may justify an extension of their claims to ridges with which they form a unit. In that way oceanic ridges could be attributed to insular states (Tonga, Samoa, Fiji, Hawaii) and even to single islands, especially if a single island forms an independent state (Nauru). Thus, a greater part of all submarine areas could be allotted to some state, and such a result would constitute inequalities on the same scale as an overall partition of the oceans which was the object of our considerations in Chapters 5 and 6.

Professor Jennings, like some other authors, also refers to the new practice of granting licenses in continental slope regions, and observes that these acts did not provoke protests from other states. But as Professor O'Connell has observed with respect to a similar situation: "protests have not been directed against the less exaggerated claims only because no State had sufficient economic interest in the matter to challenge what might be described as intention to commit wrong." [8] Normally, protests are lodged only when the interests of a state are directly affected. But in this case a resolution voted by the United Nations General Assembly—2574 D(XXIV) [9]—warns against further extensions of encroachments into submarine areas, and this is more effective than individual protests.

We conclude that claims to the continental slope are not covered by existing law, either by the provisions of the Convention on the Continental Shelf, or by customary international law. All suggestions in that sense cannot be considered as interpretations of existing law, but only as proposals *de lege ferenda*. If they succeed, the "heritage of mankind" will be reduced to areas that it will not be possible, for a long time, to exploit "for the benefit of mankind".

---

[8] O'Connell, "Sedentary Fisheries and the Australian Continental Shelf", *Am. J. Int'l L.*, 1955, p. 194.

[9] For a discussion of G. A. Res. 2574 D, see *supra*, p. 127.

# Selected Bibliography

Alexander, *Offshore Geography of Northwestern Europe,* 1963.

Alinat, "Les expériences précontinent et leurs perspectives," Conference on Petroleum and the Sea, 1965, Paper 415.

The American Assembly, *Uses of the Sea,* 1968.

Andrassy, *Epikontinentalni pojas,* 1951.

Andrassy, "Potreba dalje kodifikacije medunarodnog prava mora," *Jug. revija za med. pravo,* 1965, no. 2, pp. 163–71.

Andrassy, "Les progrès techniques et l'extension du plateau continental," *Zeitschrift für ausländisches öffentliches Recht und Völkerrecht,* vol. 26 (1966), p. 698–704.

Andrassy, *The Continental Shelf and Customary International Law,* International Problems, Belgrade, 1969.

Lord Asquith of Bishopstone, "Petroleum Development (Trucial Coast) Limited v. The Ruler of Abu Dhabi" (Award), [*1951*] *International Law Reports,* pp. 144–61. Also printed in *International and Comparative Law Quarterly,* vol. 1 (1952), pp. 247–61.

Auguste, *The Continental Shelf: The Practice and Policy of Latin American States with Special Reference to Chile, Ecuador and Peru,* 1960.

Azcárraga, "Los derechos sobre la plataforma submarina," *Revista Española de derecho internacional,* vol. 2 (1949), pp. 47–99.

Berne, "Ancrage dynamique," Conference on Petroleum and the Sea, 1965, Paper 120.

Bernfeld, "Developing the Resources of the Sea—Security of Investment," *The International Lawyer*, vol. 2 (1967), pp. 67–76.

van Bilderbeek, *Offshore Exploration, Drilling and Development*, 1965.

Boggs, "Delimitation of Seaward Areas Under National Jurisdiction," *American Journal of International Law*, vol. 45 (1951), pp. 240–66.

Bond, "Undersea Living: A New Capacity," Conference on Petroleum and the Sea, 1965, Paper 417.

Booda, "Navy Currents," *Undersea Technology*, July, 1967, p. 41.

Borgese, *The Ocean Regime*, 1968.

Bouchez, *The Regime of Bays in International Law*, 1964.

Bourcart, *Géographie des fonds des mers*, 1949.

Bourcart, "Note sur la définition des formes du terrain sous-marin," *Deep-Sea Research*, vol. 2 (January, 1955), pp. 140–44.

Bowett, *The Law of the Sea*, 1967.

Brooks, *Low-Grade and Nonconventional Sources of Manganese*, 1966.

Brown, "The Legal Regime of Inner Space: Military Aspects," *Current Legal Problems*, vol. 22 (1969), pp. 181–204.

Burke, *Ocean Sciences, Technology and the Future International Law of the Sea*, 1966.

Burke, *Towards a Better Use of the Ocean*, 1969.

Busch, "Der Festlandsockel im Schnittpunkt von Meeresfreiheit und Staatensouveränität," *Internationales Recht und Diplomatie*, 1967, pp. 79–100.

Christy, *The Common Wealth in Ocean Fisheries*, 1965.

Christy, "A Social Scientist Writes on Economic Criteria for Rules Governing Exploitation of Deep Sea Minerals," *The International Lawyer*, vol. 2 (1968), pp. 224–42.

Christy, "Alternative Regimes for the Marine Resources Underlying High Seas," *Natural Resources Lawyer*, vol. 1 (1968), pp. 63–77.

Clark, "Remote Manipulation for Sea-Floor Operation," Conference on Petroleum and the Sea, 1965, Paper 712.

Clawson (ed.), *Natural Resources and International Development: Essays from the Fifth Annual Resources for the Future Forum,* 1964.

Commission on Marine Science, Engineering and Resources, *Marine Resources and Legal-Political Arrangements for their Development,* 1969.

Commission on Marine Science, Engineering and Resources, *Our Nation at Sea,* 1969.

Commission to Study the Organization of Peace, *The United Nations and the Bed of the Sea,* 1969.

Conference of the Law of the Sea Institute, (Alexander ed.), *The Law of the Sea,* (3 vol., 1967–1969).

*Conference on Law, Organization and Security in the Use of the Sea,* (2 vol., 1967).

Cousteau, "At Home at Sea," *National Geographic,* April, 1964, pp. 465–507.

Craven, "Working in the Sea," *Science and Technology,* April 1967, p. 51.

Defant, *Physical Oceanography,* 1961.

*Developments in the Law of the Sea 1958–1964* (British Institute of International and Comparative Law, International Law Series No. 3, 1965).

Eek, "The Hydrological Cycle and the Law of Nations." *Scandinavian Studies in Law,* vol. 9 (1965), pp. 49–91.

*Effective Use of the Sea, Report of the Panel on Oceanography, President's Science Advisory Committee,* 1966.

Eichelberger, "A Case for the Administration on Marine Resources Underlying the High Seas by the United Nations," *Natural Resources Lawyer,* vol. 1 (1968), pp. 85–94.

Ely, "American Policy Options in the Development of Undersea Mineral Resources," *Natural Resources Lawyer,* vol. 1 (1968), pp. 91–95.

Fairbridge, *Encyclopedia of Oceanography,* 1966.

Fauchille, *Traité de droit international public,* I, 2, 1925.

François, "Report on the Regime of the High Seas," A/CN.4/17, *Yearbook of the International Law Commission,* 1950, II, pp. 36–113.

François, "Quatrième Rapport (Le plateau continental et les sujets voisins), A/CN.4/60, *Yearbook of the International Law Commission*, 1953, II, pp. 1–50.

Franklin, *The Law of the Sea: Some Recent Developments* (U. S. Naval War College, International Law Studies, 1959–1960), 1961.

Friedmann, "The Race to the Bottom of the Sea," *Columbia Forum*, vol. 12 (1969), pp. 18–21.

Garcia-Amador, *Exploitation and Conservation of the Resources of the Sea*, 1963.

Gaskell, *World Beneath the Oceans*, 1964.

Gidel, *Le droit international public de la mer*, 1930.

Gidel, "A propos des bases juridiques des prétentions des Etats riverains sur les plateau continental: les doctrines du droit inhérent," *Zeitschrift für ausländisches öffentliches Recht und Völkerrecht*, vol. 19 (1958), pp. 81–101.

Gilluly, Waters and Woodford, *Principles of Geology*, 1952.

Goddard, "The Narrowing Seas," *Indian Yearbook of International Affairs*, vol. 3 (1954), pp. 240–56.

Goldie, "Sedentary Fisheries and Art. 2(4) of the Continental Shelf Convention: A Plea for a Separate Regime," *American Journal of International Law*, vol. 63 (1969), pp. 86–97.

Goldie, "The Contents of Davy Jones's Locker: A Proposed Regime for the Seabed and Subsoil," *Rutgers Law Review*, vol. 22 (1968), pp. 1–66.

Goldie, "Special Regimes and Pre-Emptive Activities in International Law," *International and Comparative Law Quarterly*, vol. II (1962), pp. 670–700.

Griffin, "The Emerging Law of the Ocean Space," *The International Lawyer*, vol. I (1967), p. 548.

Griffin, "The Law of the Sea and the Continental Shelf." Address delivered before the International Academy of Trial Lawyers, February 17, 1967.

Griffin, "Routes maritimes à travers les champs pétrolifères du Golfe de Mexique," *Revue hydrographique internationale*, vol. 44 (1967), p. 195.

Grunawalt, "Acquisition of the Resources of the Bottom of the Sea:

A New Frontier of International Law." *Military Law Review,* vol. 34 (1966), pp. 101–33.

Guarino and Kojanec, "Régime juridique du plateau continental," *Revue pétrolière,* vol. 2 (1965), pp. 201 *et seq.*

Guilcher, *Morphologie littorale et sousmarine,* 1954.

Guilcher, "Continental Shelf and Slope," in Hill, *The Sea,* vol. 3 (1963).

Haight, "The Seabed and the Ocean Floor," *The International Lawyer,* vol. 3 (1969), pp. 642–73.

Hall, "Survey of a Newly Discovered Feature (Genista Bank) off the Arabian Coast," *Deep-Sea Research,* vol. 2 (1954), p. 80.

Hall, "Banc Hall—nouveau guyot dans le Canal de Mozambique," *Revue hydrographique internationale,* 1967, pp. 31–33.

Hannen, "Oxy/Helium Deep Diving Experiments and Trials," Conference on Petroleum and the Sea, 1965, Paper 410.

de Hartingh, "La position française à l'égard de la Convention de Genève sur le plateau continental," *Annuaire français de droit international,* vol. II (1965), pp. 725–34.

Henkin, *Law for the Sea's Mineral Resources,* 1968.

*Interim Report on the United Nations and the Issue of Deep Ocean Resources,* 90th Congress, 1st Session, House Report No. 999, 1967.

Hudson, "The First Conference for the Codification of International Law," *American Journal of International Law,* vol. 24 (1930), pp. 447–66.

Hull, "The Political Ocean," *Foreign Affairs,* vol. 45 (1967), pp. 492–507.

Hurst, "Whose is the Bed of the Sea?" *British Yearbook of International Law, 1923–1924,* vol. 4 (1923), pp. 34–43.

Hurst, "Problems of Peace and War," *Transactions of the Grotius Society,* vol. 34 (1948), pp. 153–69.

Ibler, *Sloboda mora (The Freedom of the Sea),* 1965.

International Institute for Peace and Conflict Research (SIPRI), *Towards a Better Use of the Oceans,* 1968. (Report by Burke and comments.)

International Law Association, *Reports* of the Conferences, 1948–1954 and 1966 *sequ.*

Johnston, "Law, Technology and the Sea." *California Law Review*, vol. 55 (1967), pp. 449–72.

Kuenen, *Marine Geology*, 1950.

Lakhtine, *Rights Over the Arctic*, 1938.

A. de Lapradelle, "Le droit de l'Etat sur la mer territoriale," *Revue générale de droit international public*, vol. 5 (1898), pp. 264–84.

A. de Lapradelle, *La mer*, 1934.

P. de Lapradelle, "La question du plateau continental," *Annales de la Faculté de droit d'Aix-en-Provence*, 1957.

Lauterpacht, "Sovereignty over Submarine Areas," *British Yearbook of International Law*, vol. 27 (1950), pp. 376–433.

Lévy, "Rechtspolitische Schwerpunkte einer Regelung der Besitz- und Nutzungsrechte des Meeresgrundes," *Oesterreichische Zeitschrift für Aussenpolitik*, vol. 8 (1968), pp. 135–48.

Lévy, "Pour un droit des fonds océaniques," *Chronique de politique étrangère*, vol. 21 (1968), pp. 721–38.

Link, "Tomorrow in the Deep Frontier," *National Geographic*, vol. 125 (1964), pp. 778–801.

Mabruk, "Offshore Oil Concession Agreements in OPEC Member Countries," Conference on Petroleum and the Sea, 1965, Paper 508.

MacChesney, *Situations, Documents and Commentary on Recent Developments in the International Law of the Sea* (U.S. Naval War College International Law Situations and Documents 1956), 1957.

McDougal and Burke, *The Public Order of the Oceans*, 1962.

McDougal and Burke, "Crisis in the Law of the Sea," *Yale Law Journal*, vol. 67 (1958), 539–89.

McKelvey and Chase, "Selecting Areas Favorable for Subsea Prospecting," *Transactions of the Second Annual Conference*, 1966, pp. 44–60.

Mallory, "Exploration of the 'Vema' Seamount," *The International Hydrographic Review*, 1966, pp. 17–23.

*Marine Science Affairs* (First Report of the President to the Congress on Marine Resources and Engineering Development, 1967).

Marine Technology Society, *Man's Extension into the Sea: Transactions of the Joint Symposium,* 1966.

Mateesco, *Le droit international nouveau,* 1948.

Menard, "Geology of the Pacific Floor," *Experientia,* vol. 15, pp. 205–13.

Menzel, *Gutachten zur Frage des kontinentalen Schelfs in der Nordsee,* 1964.

Menzel, "Der deutsche Festlandsockel in der Nordsee und seine rechtliche Ordnung," *Archiv des öffentlichen Rechts,* vol. 90 (1965), pp. 1 *et seq.*

Menzel, "Der Festlandsockel der Bundesrepublik Deutschland und das Urteil des Internationalen Gerichtshofs vom 20. Februar 1969," *Jahrbuch für internationales Recht,* vol. 14 (1969), pp. 13–100.

Mero, *The Mineral Resources of the Sea,* 1965.

Miseev, *The Present State and Perspectives for the Development of the World Fisheries,* 1964.

Mouton, "The Continental Shelf," *Recueil des cours de l'Académie de droit international à La Haye,* vol. 85 (1954), pp. 343–465.

Mouton, "Recent Developments in the Technology of Exploiting the Continental Shelf," U.N. document A/CONF.13/25.

Münch, "Legal Aspects of Drilling for and Transportation of Oil and Gas on the High Seas," *Revue pétrolière,* 1965.

National Petroleum Council, *Petroleum Resources under the Ocean Floor,* 1969. (See also *Interim Report,* 1968).

Novák, "On the Origin of the Continental Shelf," *Véstnik Královské Česke Společnosti nauk,* 1937.

*Ocean Science and Ocean Engineering* (a collection of papers, 2 vols., 1965).

O'Connell, "Sedentary Fisheries and the Australian Continental Shelf," *American Journal of International Law,* vol. 49 (1955), pp. 185–209.

Oda, *International Control of Sea Resources,* 1963.

Oda, "The Geneva Conventions: Some Suggestions to their Revision," *Natural Resources Lawyer,* vol. 1 (1968), pp. 103–14.

Oda, "Proposals for Revising the Convention on the Continental

Shelf," *Columbia Journal of Transnational Law*, vol. 7 (1968), pp. 1–31.

Oda, "Boundary of the Continental Shelf," *Japanese Annual of International Law*, vol. 12 (1968), pp. 264–84.

Odell, *The Economic Geography of Oil*, 1963.

van Panhuys and van Emde Boas, "Legal Aspects of Pirate Broadcasting," *American Journal of International Law*, vol. 60 (1966), pp. 303–41.

Pardo, "Whose is the Bed of the Sea?" *Proceedings of the American Society of International Law*, 1968, pp. 216–29.

Pardo, "Who Will Control the Seabed?" *Foreign Affairs*, vol. 47 (1968), pp. 123–37.

Pell and Goodwin, *Challenge of the Seven Seas*, 1966.

Perry (ed.), *Ocean Engineering*, 1965.

*Potential Resources of the Ocean* (Van Camp Sea Food Company, Port of Long Beach, California, 1965).

Rosenstein, *A Draft Multilateral Convention on the Use of the Deep Ocean Floor*, 1968.

Scelle, *Plateau continental et droit international*, 1955.

Schachter, "Scientific Advance and International Law Making," *California Law Review*, vol. 55 (1967), pp. 423–30.

Sears, (ed.), *Progress in Oceanography*, 1965.

Shalowitz, *Shore and Sea Boundaries*, 1962.

Shepard, *Submarine Geology*, 2nd ed. 1963.

Sohn, "Exploitation of the Sea Bed Outside the Continental Shelf" (unpublished paper).

Sørensen, "The Law of the Sea," *International Conciliation*, 1958, No. 520.

Stenuyt, "The Man in the Sea Project," Conference on Petroleum and the Sea, 1965, Paper 423.

Stride, "The Geology of Some Continental Shelves," *Oceanography and Marine Biology*, 1963.

Sverdrup, Johnson, and Fleming, *The Oceans*, 1957.

Thoulet, *Guide d'océanographie pratique*, 1895.

Tuttle, *Down Deep in the Sea*, 1968.

Weissberg, "International Law Meets the Short-Term National Interest: The Maltese Proposal on the Seabed and Ocean Floor,"

*International and Comparative Law Quarterly*, vol. 18 (1967), pp. 41–102.

World Peace Through Law Center, *Treaty Governing the Exploration and Use of the Sea Bed* (Pamphlet Series 10, 1968).

Young, "A Conceptual Design Analysis of a Completely Submersible Offshore Drilling Operation," Conference on Petroleum and the Sea, 1965, Paper 419.

Young, "The Geneva Convention on the Continental Shelf: A First Impression," *American Journal of International Law*, vol. 52 (1958), pp. 731–38.

Young, "The Legal Regime of the Deep-Sea Floor," *American Journal of International Law*, vol. 62 (1968), pp. 641–53.

Zaorski, *Ekspoatacja biologicznych zasobów morza w świetle prawa międzynarodowego* (*The Exploitation of the Biological Resources of the Sea in the Light of International Law*), 1967.

# Index of Cases

*Anglo-Norwegian Fisheries* (1951)
 adjacency, concept of, 82
 baselines, 37
*The Grisbadarna Case* (1909)
 adjacency, concept of, 81-82
*North Sea Continental Shelf Cases* (1969)
 adjacency criterion, 89
 continental shelf as prolongation of land, 113n, 170, 172
 customary international law, Geneva Convention as, 66-67
 delimitation by negotiation, 92, 94
 equidistance principle, application of, 89, 94, 96-99
 map of North Sea, 97
*Petroleum Development (Trucial Coast) Ltd. v. The Ruler of Abu Dhabi* (1951)
 legal status of continental shelf, 59-60

# Index

Banks, 11-13
Bays, as internal waters, 38-39
Bernfeld, Seymour S., on delimitation, 107
Brajkovic, V., on limits of continental shelf, 74

Canada, disarmament proposal, 151
Center for the Study of Democratic Institutions, proposal for international regime, 159-60, 163-65
Ceylon, claims to fisheries, 47
Chile, claims to maritime zones, 42-44
    exploitability criterion, on, 85
Committee (Eighteen Nation) on Disarmament, activities of, 149-53
Committee of Experts for the Progressive Codification of International Law (1925), proposals on continental shelf, 71
Contiguous zones, 46-48
Continental margin, relation to continental shelf, 169-74
    defined, 4
Continental rise, 4
Continental shelf, area of, 4n
    Convention on, see Conventions, treaties, etc.

customary international law, status in, 56-69
definition, legal in relation to scientific, 52-53, 71-72, 113-14
definition, scientific, 3-10
delimitation, see Delimitation of continental shelf
islands, 103-105
maps of, 6-7, 97, 100-101
Mediterranean seas, 4n, 105-106
origins, 10-11
Continental slope, definition, 4
profile, 9
Conventions, treaties, etc.: Convention for the Regulation of the Police of the Fisheries in the North Sea, 39
Danish-German Agreement of June 9, 1965, 93n
Declaration of Santiago on the Maritime Zone, 42-43
European Fisheries Convention, 93
Geneva Convention on the Continental Shelf, customary international law, relation to, 53-63
    delimitation by, see delimitation of continental shelf

Conventions, treaties, etc. (*Continued*)
   legal consequences of, 63-69, 171-72
   provisions of, 55, 91-92, 94n
   revision of, proposals, 117-28
Geneva Convention on Fishing and Conservation of Living Resources of the High Seas, 47-48, 102
Geneva Convention on the High Seas, 55, 102
Geneva Convention on the Territorial Sea and the Contiguous Zones, 36, 37-42, 45-46, 55, 68, 152
London Convention for the Prevention of Pollution of the Sea by Oil, 47
Customary law, relation to Geneva Convention on Continental Shelf, 53-69
Cyprus, proposal on deep seabed, 126

Dean, Arthur H., on exploitability criterion, 80
Delimitation of continental shelf, adjacency criterion, 81-82, 87-90, 119, 124, 172
   base lines, 36, 38, 39-40
   Denmark, continental shelf, delimitation of, 93n, 96-99
   equidistance (median line) criterion, 91-98
   exploitability criterion, adoption of, 72n, 73-76, 77-78
      elastic nature of, 84-85, 122
      international attitudes toward, 120-21
      limits to, 87-90, 124, 172
      meaning of, 78-81, 82-90
   fixed-width criterion, 76-77, 117-20
   geological criteria, 71-73, 76, 113-14
   isobath criterion, advantages of, 77, 114, 172
      generally, 77, 112-20
      international attitudes toward, 121-22
   status as customary law, 67-69

Developed countries, attitudes toward international regime, 156-57
   "Flag state" approach, 131-32
Developing countries, attitudes towards international regime, 79-80, 121-22
   benefits from, 138-40
Disarmament proposals, 146-54
Driessen, C.F., on limits of continental shelf, 74, 85n

Ecuador, claim to maritime zone, 42-44
Elevations and oceanic shallows, 11
European Fisheries Convention, 93
Extraction of resources, 22-27, 84, 85n

Fauchille, Paul, on nature of territorial sea, 45
Fisheries, 16, 47-48, 93
"Flag state" approach to asserting jurisdiction, 131-32
France, position on continental shelf, 73-74, 88, 96, 96n
François, J.P.A., on status and delimitation of continental shelf, 52, 62, 72, 77
Franklin, Carl M. on Geneva Convention on Continental Shelf as codifying law, 63

Garcia-Amador, on Santiago Declaration, 44
Germany, delimitation of continental shelf, 93n, 97, 98
   proposal for international regime, 135
Ghana, claim to fishing zone, 47
   position on international seabed regime, 122, 155
Gidel, G., on limits of continental shelf, 74, 85n
Grotius, Hugo, definition of internal waters by, 37
Guarino and Kojanec, proposal for international regime, 135
Guinea, claim to fisheries zone, 47

Henkin, Louis, on exploitability criterion, 78*n*, 82
proposal for delimitation, 119, 115*n*
Honduras, claims to maritime zones, 44
Hsu, Shuhsi, proposal for international regime, 133
Hudson, Manley O., on continental shelf, 61, 72*n*

Iceland, proposal on shelf delimitation, 73-74
India, claim to fisheries zone, 47
Indonesia, continental shelf of, 104, 106
territorial sea of, 40
Institut de Droit International, proposals on territorial waters, 39, 45
on international regime, 132*n*
Internal Waters, 37-39
International Coffee Organization, structure of, 162-63
International Law Association, studies on continental shelf, 51-53, 60, 115, 146*n*
International Law Commission, continental shelf, draft articles on, 54, 66-68, 71-78, 83-88, 171
function of, 54
International regime for the seabed, criteria of, 154-55
examples of models of organization, 159-65
functions, 165-66
internationalization of continental shelf, 134
membership in, 158-59
necessity of, 129-32
proposals for, 132-46, 155-58
Iran, attitude toward international regime, 155
Islands continental shelf of, 103-105
territorial sea of 39-40
Israel, position of on continental shelf, 59

Jamaica, position on exploitability criterion, 79-80

Japan, position on international regime, 155
Jennings, R.Y., on North Sea Continental Shelf Cases, 170-74

el Khoury, Faris Bey, on delimitation of continental shelf, 73
Kojanec and Guarino, proposals for international regime, 135
Kojevnikov, F.J., on definition of continental shelf, 72-73

Landlocked Countries, position of, 102-103
de Lapradelle, Albert, on territorial sea, 45, 46*n*
proposals on international regime, 133
de Lapradelle, Paul, proposal on international regime, 135
Lauterpacht, H., on legal status of continental shelf, 56-58
Liberia, proposal for international regime, 156
Luce, Charles F., on accessibilty of resources, 23-26

Malta, position on delimitation of continental shelf, 119-20
proposals for international regime, 123, 126, 127-28, 137-40, 155
Mauritius, proposal on international regime, 126
Mediterranean seas, continental shelf of, 4*n*, 105-106
Military uses of the seabed, devices and techniques, 21-22
disarmament, 146-54
Mouton, M.W., on the continental shelf, 61, 74
on exploitability criterion, 73*n*, 85*n*
Myrdal, A., proposal for international regime, 156

Natural resources, *see* Resources of the sea
Netherlands, proposals for international regime, 133-34

Nixon, Richard M., disarmament proposal, 151
North Sea, division of continental shelf, 88-89, 93$n$, 96-99
fisheries regulation, 39
map, 97
Norway, delimitation of North Sea, 88-89
position on continental shelf, 59

O'Connell, D.P., on acquiescence in claims, 65$n$, 173-74

Pakistan, claim to fisheries zone, 47
Pell, Claiborne, on delimitation of continental shelf, 116
proposals for international regime, 145, 146$n$
Peru, claims to maritime zones, 42, 43
Pollution, of the seas, 47, 141

Resources of the sea, acquiculture, 20-21
definition, 16
fisheries, sedentary, 16
minerals, 18-20
oil and natural gas, 17, 84, 85$n$

Santiago Declaration (on the Maritime Zone), 42-44
Scelle, George, position on status of continental shelf, 61, 72
Seabed, defined, 3
division of, hypothetical, 99-107
map, 100-101
Sierra Leone, proposal for international regime, 155-56
shallows and oceanic elevations, 11-13
Sorenson, Max, on status of continental shelf, 26$n$
South Africa, on delimitation of continental shelf, 73-74, 85
Submarine activity, 20-31
Subsoil of seabed, defined, 3
resources of, *see* Resources of the sea

Sweden, position on continental shelf, 58-59, 155-56

Tanzania, proposals on continental shelf, 126, 150
Technology, present capability and projects, 21-31, 85$n$, 165$n$
relation to exploitability criterion, 78-81
Territorial Sea, extension of, 38-39, 40-45, 68
nature of, 45-46
Transportation, underwater, 27-28
Treaties, *see* Conventions, treaties, etc.
Truman, Harry S., Proclamation on Continental Shelf, 49-50, 171
Turkey, proposal for international regime, 156

Underdeveloped countries, *see* Developing countries
UNIDO, structure of, 160-61
Union of Soviet Socialist Republics, disarmament proposals, 148$n$, 149-52
proposals for international regime, 137, 156-57
protest, special fishing zone, 47
United Kingdom, adjacency, 88
boundaries in North Sea, 89, 97
delimitation of continental shelf, 73-74, 93, 95
position on status of continental shelf, 59
United Nations, Committee (Eighteen-Nation) on Disarmament, 149-53
Development Program, structure, 161-62
disarmament efforts, 146-54
ECOSOC, study of sea resources, 136
General Assembly, First Committee, 120-22, 139, 141
resolutions adopted, on interna-

tional regime for seabed, 127, 128, 136-37, 139-40, 141-42, 143-44, 156-57
on disarmament, 147, 153
Industrial Development Organization, (UNIDO), structure, 160-61
International Law Commission, *see* International Law Commission
Secretary General, reports of, 136, 137, 156
Seabed Committees, activities of, 119-20, 128, 139-43
United States, adjacency test, 88
disarmament proposals, 149-52
exploitability test, 86
seabed proposals before Congress, 116, 145-46
Truman Proclamation, 50

Uruguay, proposal for international regime, 126

Villamil, Lopez, on Santiago Declaration, 44

Waldock, C.H.M., on delimitation of continental shelf, 74
Whiteman, Marjorie, on exploitability criterion, 86

Yepes, J.M., on legal status of continental shelf, 58
Young, R.Y., on exploitability criterion, 79n
Yugoslavia, delimitation of continental shelf, 73-74, 95
proposals for international regime, 146n, 157